68172

MUSIC ENGRAVING
AND PRINTING

Da Capo Press Music Reprint Series
GENERAL EDITOR
FREDERICK FREEDMAN
VASSAR COLLEGE

MUSIC ENGRAVING AND PRINTING

Historical and Technical Treatise

BY

WILLIAM GAMBLE

𝄞 DA CAPO PRESS • NEW YORK • 1971

A Da Capo Press Reprint Edition

This Da Capo Press edition of
Music Engraving and Printing
is an unabridged republication of the first
edition published in London in 1923.

Library of Congress Catalog Card Number 70-155576

SBN 306-70168-5

Published by Da Capo Press, Inc.
A Subsidiary of Plenum Publishing Corporation
227 West 17th Street, New York, N. Y. 10011
All Rights Reserved

Manufactured in the United States of America

*For Distribution and Sale Only in the
United States of America*

MUSIC ENGRAVING
AND PRINTING

MUSIC ENGRAVING AND PRINTING

Historical and Technical Treatise

BY

WILLIAM GAMBLE, F.O.S., F.R.P.S.

EDITOR OF "THE PROCESS YEAR BOOK,"
AUTHOR OF "LINE PHOTO-ENGRAVING," "PHOTOGRAPHY
AND ITS APPLICATIONS," ETC.

LONDON
SIR ISAAC PITMAN & SONS, LTD.
PARKER STREET, KINGSWAY, W.C.2
BATH, MELBOURNE, TORONTO, NEW YORK
1923

PREFACE

SOON after the beginning of the late war the Author was led to make an investigation into the position of the music printing industry and the causes of its decadence in this country. The circumstances which prompted this investigation were that statements were being made at that time in the Press concerning the extent to which we had been dependent on Germany for musical publications. Not only had a vast amount of music printing been imported here in the form of editions of the works of composers of international fame, but British musical compositions were largely sent to Germany to be engraved and printed. When public protest was raised some time before the war, and it seemed likely that some form of protective tariff might be instituted, some of the large German firms established works in this country, thus further cutting out the British music engravers and printers. The result was that purely British work in this line of industry diminished to almost a vanishing point.

This was all the more to be regretted, because at one time English music engravers excelled those of any other nation. Fifty or sixty years ago they were able to keep British music work in our own country, but gradually the position was changed until Germany had an almost complete monopoly of engraved and lithographed music.

This was a galling reflection to the patriotic mind, but still more so was the fact that the majority of British music professors expressed a preference for the German-printed music, and its undoubted excellence made it difficult to gainsay this preference.

It was remarked by a musical writer at the outbreak of war that many thousands of amateurs, apart from professional musicians, would be aghast at the idea of being deprived of the German musical publications. However, the war compelled them to do without such works, and it is to be hoped the desire to possess them will never again arise. Nor will it if British music printers have risen to the opportunity offered to them during the war.

We have revealed in the last chapter of this book some of the causes which led to the decadence of British music engraving and printing, and we have tried to indicate how these causes can be removed. Perhaps some of the difficulties of the business have been surmounted owing to the necessities created by war conditions, and certainly a good deal more work is now being done by British firms. They have their opportunity to recover entirely the lost ground of pre-war time, and it would be unfortunate if the chance has not been fully grasped.

In the course of investigation, the Author was led to believe that one reason for so much work going abroad was the lack of information on the subject of music engraving and printing. In most industries, the publication of technical books explaining crafts and processes has stimulated trade and infused new ideas, and it is in the hope that such will be the effect of the present book on the music printing industry. So far, there has been no book in the English language on the subject, and only a small *brochure* in French. There seemed, therefore, an opening for a complete treatise, and this the Author has endeavoured to supply.

It has not been an easy task, and the preparation of the book has extended over a long period. It was necessary to obtain most of the technical information by personally interviewing those in the trade, and the Author desires to acknowledge the kind readiness to assist manifested by all to whom he applied. Where so many have helped, it is impossible to express acknowledgments individually ; but, as far as possible, reference has been made in the text to the sources of information.

One exception must be made in the matter of individual acknowledgment. The Author was fortunate in securing the assistance of Mr. Leonard Groves, the instructor in music engraving at the London School of Arts and Crafts. This gentleman has taken great pains in reading through the manuscript of the chapters on the technique of music engraving, and has suggested many useful corrections and additions. He was also good enough to assist in the preparation of the illustrations of the tools and the methods of handling them, as well as examples showing stages of the work. Coming from such an experienced and skilful engraver, the information will be found thoroughly practical and reliable.

It is hoped by the Author that the book will stimulate interest in the subject not only amongst engravers and printers, but also members of the musical profession, so that the latter, by means of a better knowledge of the methods of music printing, will be more sympathetic towards the efforts of the trade in this country to raise their craft to a higher level and thus prevent the work from ever again falling into foreign hands.

CONTENTS

CONTENTS —(*contd.*)

PART I

HISTORICAL NOTES ON THE RISE AND PROGRESS OF MUSIC ENGRAVING AND PRINTING

MUSIC ENGRAVING AND PRINTING

CHAPTER I

THE REPRESENTATION OF MUSICAL SOUNDS

APPARENTLY the idea of representing musical sounds by written signs must be ascribed to the Greeks, but as they owed the essentials of their knowledge on most subjects to the Egyptians, it is possible that the origin dates back to a still earlier period. It is true that neither a scrap of Egyptian music nor a single theoretical treatise has come down to us, but the most ancient tombs and rocks show representations of musical instruments of elaborate construction.

Dr. Burney, after a lifelong research into the musical notations of ancient nations, thus summarizes the result of his efforts—

It does not appear from history that the Egyptians, Phoenicians, and Hebrews, or any ancient people who cultivated the arts, except the Greeks and the Romans, had musical characters, and these had no symbols of sound other than the letters of the alphabet, which likewise served for alphabetical numbers and chronological dates.

It may be said that the musical notation is as old

as the alphabet, for that is as far as our knowledge goes ; and the Greeks were the earliest to make use of this principle. They used uncial letters intermixed with a few menisculae, and written in an endless variety of different positions. Some were upright, some inverted, others lying on the right or left side, and variously grouped, but all falling into a system containing about 120 well-marked combinations, with minor variations running into about a thousand. Although the system has been so clearly described by many Hellenic writers, it is a singular fact that not a scrap of ancient Greek music exists, unless we accept three fragments whose authenticity is thought to be doubtful. Supposition ascribes these to the third or fourth century.

What we know of the system is chiefly derived from treatises on the subject by the old Greek philosophers, Alypius, Aristides, Quintillianus, and others ; and their explanations are so clear that it has been said if we could but obtain copies of the hymns of Pindar or the choruses of Sophocles, it would probably be easier to decipher them than many mediaeval manuscripts.

There were two sets of signs employed in Greek music—one for the voice and the other for the instrument. The first were the letters of the alphabet, and the second are supposed to be adapted from the cabalistic signs of the heavenly bodies.

We give an example from Grove's *Dictionary of Music* of the Greek music with the corresponding signs in present date notation.

Though the Romans borrowed the Greek scale,

4

they did not adopt the whole of the complicated system. They took the first fifteen letters of their alphabet, A to P, and gave Latin names to each of the letters.

Boëthius, writing in the sixth century, sanctions the use of the fifteen letters for certain special purposes, but the system gradually fell into disuse, and the number was reduced to seven : it is not easy to

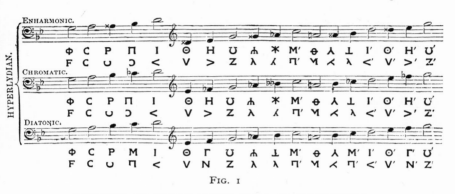

FIG. 1

EXAMPLE OF GREEK MUSIC WITH CORRESPONDING
MODERN NOTATION

say by whom. Tradition ascribes the use of the lesser number to St. Gregory, but on quite insufficient grounds.

Pope Gregory I (known as Gregory the Great, or Saint Gregory) is usually credited with the introduction of what is known as Gregorian music, and his autograph MS. music-book is chained to the altar at St. Peter's, Rome. He certainly ordained a ritual dated A.D. 590, which was called Gregorian, but it was not the system of music now known by that

5

name. This system actually came into use some centuries later.

If we are to believe St. Isidore, the friend and survivor of Gregory, no music of the period of this Roman pontiff was, or could be, preserved, for in one of his works this authority says—

Unless sounds are retained in the memory, they perish, because they cannot be written.

The system ascribed to Gregory is that of representing the different sounds by the first seven letters of the Roman alphabet. What probably is the fact is that someone during his pontifical reign discovered that the sounds represented by the last seven letters of the scale of fifteen in the Roman notation, as borrowed from the Greeks, was but a repetition of the first seven A to H, and Gregory was asked to give his authority to the first seven only being used, as tending to simplification. The last eight letters were accordingly abolished, and the first seven were used over again, the lower octave being expressed by capitals and the upper by small letters. Thus—

A	B	C	D	E	F	G		a	b	c	d	e	f	g
la	si	do	re	mi	fa	sol		la	si	do	re	mi	fa	sol

Though we have placed under the letters the sounds corresponding to them, it will be seen in a later portion of this chapter that the name of the sounds did not come into use until some centuries after.

It is not really easy to fix any period when letters came to be used and when they fell into disuse. They were used for many centuries in the notation of plain chant in the West, just as the Greek characters were retained in the Office Book of the Eastern Church. After the eighth century, though they rarely appeared in writing, the degrees of the scale were still named after them, and as symbols of these degrees they have never been discarded. Long before the invention of the stave, the system of using alphabetical letters came to an end, but it survives in our own day in the nomenclature of the notes, and in the employment of the F, C, and G clefs.

Though this system of using letters was not wanting in clearness nor in certainty, it had the serious defect of being a mere collection of arbitrary signs, arranged in straight lines above the poetical text, without attempting to imitate in some symmetrical form the undulations of the melody represented.

To remedy this defect, a new system was brought into use, based on an entirely different principle and introducing an entirely new set of characters, of which the first well-formed examples are to be found in the MSS. of the eighth century, though it is believed by some authorities that the signs can be traced back as far as the sixth century. This series of signs were called *neumae* or *neumes*. The very origin of the word is doubtful. It may be from νεῦμα (a nod *or* sign), or, as some suppose, from πνεῦμα (pneuma *or* pneumata) [literally, breaths]. The latter is the usually accepted explanation, though the former is quite as likely if we suppose that the signs represented the nods or beats of the conductor. The word may, however, have arisen from the " pneuma" or long succession of notes sung after a plain chant " Alleluia."

The characters used consisted of dots, lines, accents,

7

hooks, curves, angles, wavy signs, etc., in seemingly innumerable shapes, bewildering at first sight, but no doubt as easy to read as our modern notation when once learnt. It was the shorthand of music, and out of it, as we shall show, originated most of the present forms of our notes.

An example is here given showing some of these *neumes*, with their signification in the modern musical notation. (Fig. 2.)

The shapes of the neumes varied with the styles of

FIG. 2

NEUMES OF THE TENTH AND ELEVENTH CENTURIES WITH THEIR SIGNIFICATION IN THE MODERN NOTATION

handwriting and according to national characteristics in writing, though they were always easy to recognize.

The example we give (Fig. 3), taken from an old German Church music-book of the fifteenth century, shows the way in which the neumes were expressed in Gothic handwriting. The usual way of writing the neumes is given underneath.

The peculiar form of the neumes still survives in modern music in the signs of the *trille*, the *grupetto*, and the *arpeggio*, which retain the last traces of the forms of the old signs. The " turn " is also a sign derived from the neumes.

The origin of the neumes can be traced from the

8

Greek accents, which were placed over or under the syllables of the words to indicate the rising and falling of the voice, and to show where the breath should be taken (as is now often done in books on elocution to lay stress on certain syllables). They were later employed separately from the words, being placed above or below a red or orange line, and afterwards between two or more lines, the spaces between indicating approximately the intervals. The lines were

FIG. 3

THE NEUMES IN GOTHIC AND ORDINARY STYLE

also made to denote pitch: a red line being used for the sign corresponding to the note F and a yellow one for C.

The neumes were thus the first step towards the modern staff notation. The transition to four stave lines and three spaces, and eventually to five lines with four spaces, as used in the present day, was rational and of obvious utility.

When the Roman notation was adopted, the stave consisted of four lines, at the head of which were placed one of the seven letters for determining the pitch of the sounds, the other notes ascending or

9

descending therefrom according to the alphabetical order of the seven letters of the scale.

Byzantine scales were used in the early Greek Church music, and are described in Byremius's *Harmonicon*, a work written about 1320. These scales are four in number and were reckoned upwards —unlike the Greek, which were reckoned downwards. The notes were named after the first seven letters of the Greek alphabet, but A was placed where our C is.

The method of using the Greek letters was introduced into the Western Church by Ambrose ; and when afterwards the first seven letters of the Latin alphabet were substituted for the Greek, the old pitch meaning was retained, and it was not till about the year 900 that the note which we call C was so named. The pitch meaning of the letters remained somewhat arbitrary until the tenth century.

Eventually, something like our present stave was employed, but the spaces only, not the lines, were used, the syllables being placed in the higher or lower of these spaces to denote to what extent the melody should rise or fall.

It is interesting here to mention that the five-line stave was not universally used even after its introduction, for some examples of ancient music types in the possession of the University Press, Oxford, show 6-, 7-, 8-, and 9-line staves, as shown by the examples here reprinted by courtesy of the Controller of the Press. These are from a book entitled *Notes on a Century of Typography at the University Press, Oxford*, by Horace Hart. (Fig. 4.)

It will be seen that both lines and spaces are here

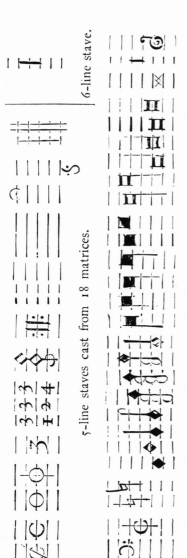

5-line staves cast from 18 matrices.

6-line stave.

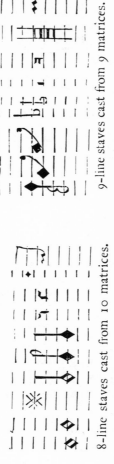

7-line staves cast from 27 matrices.

8-line staves cast from 10 matrices.

9-line staves cast from 9 matrices.

FIG. 4

ANCIENT MUSIC TYPES (SOURCE UNKNOWN) IN THE POSSESSION OF THE
OXFORD UNIVERSITY PRESS

11

utilized. This was a further step in the progress of the musical notation, and was the feature of the plain-song which survives to the present day. In this system, some one line of the stave is marked by a special letter C, D, F, or G, and the rest of the seven letters are in the order assigned to the other lines and to the spaces in the stave in forward rotation when ascending and backwards in descending. (Fig. 5.)

We see from the foregoing paragraph the origin of the system of clefs. It may here be explained why

A   B   C   D   E   F   G   a   b   b   a   G   F   E   D   C   B   A

Fig. 5

THE GREGORIAN SCALE

these signs are called clefs (sometimes written " cliff " in old musical works). *Clef* is the French word for key, and is derived from the Latin word *clavis*, also denoting key. The Germans use the word *schlussel*, which also means key. Thus the letter used as the clef becomes, as its name implies, the keynote. It requires a considerable stretch of imagination, how-ever, to see in the shape of the modern clefs any resemblance to the letters they represent. But it must be remembered that the present forms of the clefs have originated from grotesque ornamental changes in the writing of the original letters used to represent them. They have attained to their pre-sent shape by successive deformation, as can be traced in the following illustrations. (Figs. 6–9.)

The bass clef is a modification of the old Gothic letter 𝕱, which in course of centuries has arrived at

12

its present shape, resembling a c. (Fig. 6.) If the sign is turned the opposite way, as is often seen in modern music, the steps of the transition can be more easily traced back to the source.   One essential feature of the sign has been preserved, namely, the two dots on each side of the line on which the clef stands.

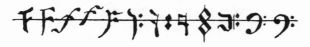

FIG. 6

TRANSITION OF THE F CLEF

Since the beginning of the eighteenth century, this clef has occupied the fourth line exclusively, but up to that time it was occasionally found on the third line, indicating that the music following it was for the baritone voice.   At a still earlier period this clef was sometimes placed on the fifth line, indicating a *basso profundo* stave.

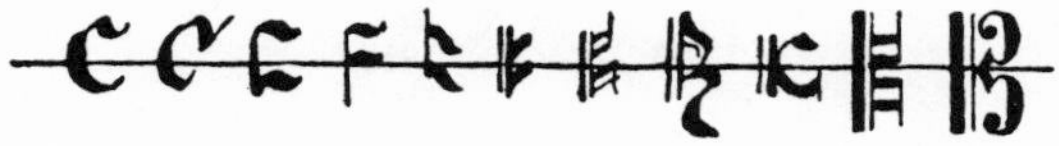

FIG. 7

TRANSITION OF THE C CLEF

The transition of the C clef from the old Gothic form is even more curious than that through which the F clef has passed.   In Fig. 7 the changes can be traced, but the form of the original letter has been entirely lost.   It now survives in forms shown in Fig. 8. These always indicate the middle C, and the line on which the clef stands is enclosed by the two diagonal

13

lines in the first form of the sign, or goes through the centre of the bracket-shaped curve in the other form. At one time or another, this sign has been placed on every line of the stave, and is now commonly used in three different places, being loosely termed the

C Clef,

FIG. 8

MODERN FORMS OF C CLEF

soprano, alto, and tenor clef, according to its position ; but different portions of the stave are arranged round it, so that, strictly speaking, its relative position remains the same.

The G or treble clef is more easily traced through

FIG. 9

CHANGES IN FORM OF THE G CLEF

its changes, having suffered less deformation than the others. Here the old Gothic letter ᶃ is the basis, and the other forms are probably turns of the pen by different writers of MS. music, the shape resulting probably from the nature of the pen used and the position of the hand in writing.

The large curve of the G clef is always placed on the first line of the stave.

In early musical MSS. it is to be noted that two and even three different clefs are sometimes found

14

on the same stave. Two other clefs may be met with in early music, d″ and G. These have now been long obsolete, but the latter survives in the use of the Greek capital letter gamma (Γ), and is used to represent the lowest sound of the musical system. From it is derived the word *gamut.*

Other interesting survivals of the old system are the sign ℭ for common time and ℭ̸ for *alla breve* time. These signs do not represent the letter " c," but the unbarred and barred semicircle of the complicated old system of rhythmic notation.

The rests for a considerable number of bars, the repetition signs, and the staccato points are also interesting to trace from the ancient music to the present notation.

When the stave came fully into use, the neumes were gradually abandoned and replaced by dots of

FIG. 10

ELEMENTS OF THE FIRST NOTES

square or lozenge form, which were thus the elements of the first notes. (Fig. 10.)

The way the names of the notes originated is an interesting story. A Benedictine monk, Guy d'Arezzo or, as he is sometimes called, Guido Aretinus, of the monastery of Pomposa, not far from Ferrara and Ravenna, is said to have invented the names " Do, Re, Mi, Fa, Sol, La, and Si " for the seven notes of the scale. He lived between the years 995 and 1050, and a great many inventions and improvements in the musical system are ascribed to him. There is a portrait of him in the refectory of the monastery of Avellana bearing the inscription "Beatus Guido inventor musicæ." Like most inventors, he had to suffer for his idea, the practical method of the system awakening the jealousy of the Abbot and his brother monks, so that he had to leave the cloister. The fame of his invention, however, reached the Pope of that time, John XIX or XX, who called him to Rome to explain the method. Guido completely triumphed through this august recognition. The Pope himself tried the method, and in the first lesson was able to find the tone of an Antiphon and to sing it.

The system was called "Solmisation," and consisted at first of the use of six syllables: "Ut re, mi, fa, sol, la." These were derived from the first syllables of the Vesper hymn for the feast of St. John the Baptist. Each line of the melody begins one note higher than the previous line, the first note being C. The words of the hymn are as follows, and the derivation of the syllables will be readily seen by noting the italics—

Ut queant laxis
*Re*sonare fibris
*Mi*ra gestorum
*Fa*muli tuorum
*Sol*ve polluti
*La*bii reatum
Sancte Ioannes.

Freely translated, the words are, in English—

That thy servants may
With resonant strings
Make apparent
Thy wondrous arts:
Absolve of pollution
The offence of the lips,
O Holy John.

It will be seen that the syllables, taken in order, are—

Ut, Re, Mi, Fa, Sol, La.

The syllable "Si" was not at first used, and the seventh note of the scale had no name. It was always

FIG. 11

Ancient Notation, with Transcription in Modern Music

THE HYMN OF ST. JOHN

represented by the letter B until the end of 1550, when the Flemish musician Waelrant gave to it the name of "Si," taken from the initial letters of the last two words of the hymn, "Sancte Iohannes."

17

The syllable *Ut* will be unfamiliar to most present-day students of music ; it corresponds to *Do* in the notation of to-day, and was substituted for *Ut* towards the end of the seventeenth century by Doni, of Florence, who held that "Ut" was a syllable too hard and difficult to sound.

The originality of D'Arezzo's invention is questioned by some German authorities on musical research. Weber says, in his *History of Indian Literature*, that the earliest mention of the seven notes of the musical scale occurs in the Vedangas, the Chandas, and the Siksha, the designation of the seven notes by the initial letters of their names being given. According to Van Bohlen in *Das Alte Indien*, and Benfey in *Ersch & Grüber's Encyclopedia*, this notation passed from the Hindus to the Persians, and from these again to the Arabs, and was introduced into European music by D'Arezzo at the beginning of the eleventh century.

Corresponding to the Indian scale "Sa, ri, ga, ma, pa, dha, ni," we have, in Persian, along with the designation of the notes by the first seven letters of the alphabet—A to G—the scale "Da, re, mi, fa, sa, la, be." These correspond very closely to the seven syllables used to-day.

As a matter of fact, the sounds are probably as old as human speech, and the syllables were the phonetic expression of the sounds. They were probably carried from the East to the West by pilgrim or crusader.

Thus far, we have traced the origin of the shapes of the notes and signs, the changes they have undergone, and the names applied to them. The next step of progress was in the fourteenth century, when Guillaume Dufay, a Fleming, one of the great masters from whom modern music has sprung, improved the notation by adding white notes to complete the series of values, and each one of them possessed an equivalent rest. (Fig. 12.)

The sign for the accidentals was introduced at a later period in the development of the notation. The " flat " is seen in a manuscript dated A.D. 930. The " sharp " first appears about the end of the thirteenth

Maxime Longue Brève Semi- Minime Semi- Fusa
Brève   Minime

FIG. 12

THE NOTATION OF GUILLAUME DUFAY

century, and the " natural " about the year 1650. The division into bars was not seen until about the year 1530.

It will be seen from the foregoing remarks that the development of the musical notation has been a matter of slow growth, the names and shapes of the notes and their placing on the stave being originated as necessity demanded for clearness and ease of reading.

The importance of being able to represent musical sounds by means of a universal notation has been realized throughout the history of music, and the modern view is well expressed in a book entitled

What is Music? by H. Heathcote Statham, from which we quote the following passage—

All important compositions are written out in musical notation, and can thus be studied and analysed at leisure by those who are able to realize in the ear of the mind (so to speak) the effects represented by the notation. To be able to do this, however, is to be an accomplished musician. Few amateurs can hope to acquire more than the power to form a general idea of the style and character of a composition from the study of the written notes. But the faculty of being able to represent sounds, their pitch and duration by written signs is vital to the art of music ; without it there could never, in fact, have been any art of music worth speaking of, and the modern system of notation, considering that it grew up and developed spontaneously, and not according to any deliberately planned scheme, is one of the most remarkable things connected with music. It has been foolishly criticized sometimes as presenting unnecessary difficulties to the learner, but no one with any natural musical ability ever found any difficulty in learning it, and others might as well let it alone. It has the immense advantage of presenting a picture to the eye of the sounds intended for the ear ; their difference of pitch, their duration, their harmonic combinations are pictorially represented and can be taken in at a glance. It is difficult to imagine any deliberately devised system which could combine so many merits, and the man who wants to invent a new system of notation may be at once dismissed as a " crank." He might as well propose to translate all the literature of the world into Esperanto.

In the early days of the musical art, the only way of duplicating music was by hand-copying, and this was naturally done by the monks of mediaeval times. The copyist of that day was an artist who sought to make his work as pleasing as possible in appearance. He used parchment at first as his material to write upon, and, later, a fine quality of hand-made paper ; and his ink was of so permanent a nature, that in most cases it has endured in its blackness to the present day. The manuscript was ornamented with

20

beautifully designed initial letters, employing gold and colour freely, so that the musical page, whilst being clear and legible, was delightful to the eye. Many of these charming old manuscript music books are to be seen in the British Museum, in the libraries of old colleges, and in the ancient cathedrals and monasteries. Some of these music books are very large, with bold characters, the explanation of this being that the music book was placed on a stand in front of the choristers when practising, so that all could see it at the same time, for naturally the making of a separate copy for each singer in the days before the invention of printing was impracticable. A picture is extant showing a choir practising in these early times, and the men are placed in such positions that all are able to read the music in the large open book on the stand in front of them.

The copyist of to-day (says E. Austin in a pamphlet entitled *The Story of the Art of Music Printing*), who has often to copy 500 pages of band-parts from full score in a week or ten days, must surely envy the copyist monks of old sitting in their gardens peacefully working to produce beautiful manuscripts. The sickening speed and difficult deciphering of careless genius-like written scores, known only too well to the badly-paid copyist of to-day, were unknown to the monks of old. It is not recorded whether any copyist-monk ever contracted writer's cramp ; whereas few copyists of to-day escape it. The duplication of music by hand lasted for centuries, and it was not until word-printing was invented that music-printing became possible.

CHAPTER II

THE ORIGIN AND PROGRESS OF TYPOGRAPHIC
MUSIC PRINTING

THE year 1465 is given as the date when printing began to supersede manuscript music. Letterpress printing had been invented or first employed in Europe either in 1438 or 1442 ; the exact date is disputed. It was not, however, until the beginning of the fifteenth century that the art was applied to anything more important than the introduction of a few notes in the psalters and service books, and even for long after this the art of music printing remained, in England at least, very far behind the progress made in other branches of typography.

At first, the new method was only utilized to the extent of printing the staves in red ink from a woodcut, the notes being written in by hand in black ink, or added by means of a stencil. In some cases the plan was reversed, the notes being written first and the red lines ruled or printed in afterwards. Evidently the stave lines were not considered essential in those days, for they were sometimes omitted.

At first the notes and staves were engraved separately on wood blocks, and the next stage of progress was the cutting of the stave lines and notes on the same block, so that they might be printed at one operation. The earliest known example of

22

this method is the work of Hans Froschauer, printed at Augsburg in 1473.

Another early example of such wood block printing is a work entitled *Musices Oposculum*, by Nicholas Burtius, printed in Bologna in 1487. A copy of this work is in the library of Mr. A. H. Littleton, and we are able to give a facsimile reproduction of it, showing what a quaintly rough piece of work it is. (Fig. 13.) [1]

The invention of printing from movable type, that is to say separate characters, is generally reckoned to date from the year 1450, when John Gutenberg, at Mentz, produced cut metal types, and used them in printing the earliest edition of the Latin Bible (termed the Mazarin, from the discovery of a copy in the Cardinal's library). We have mentioned the block printing of a later date because there are no records of music printed from movable type of an earlier date than the block printing, if we except a work printed in 1473, in Germany, by a printer named Gerson. This is a lengthy theological work, but only contains five notes of music which are evidently printed from separate characters. Small as this example is, it actually forms the foundation of music printing.

In 1482, Caxton, the first English printer, produced a book entitled *Policronicon*, by Ralph Higden, a monk of St. Werbergh's, Chester ; and in this are a few notes of music. Caxton evidently had no type for the musical notes, so he left a space for them to be filled in by hand. A copy of this work in the British Museum shows this space left clear,

---

[1] The illustrations, Figs. 13, 14, 15, are kindly lent by Messrs. Lowe & Buydone, who published them in a pamphlet, *The Story of Music Printing*.

FIG. 13

AN EXAMPLE OF COMPLETE WOOD BLOCK PRINTING

Page from *Musices Oposculum* of Burtius, 1487

the filling-in of the music having evidently been forgotten.

Wynkyn de Worde, who succeeded Caxton, reprinted Higden's work in 1495, ingeniously solving the difficulty of filling in the musical notes by using inverted types printing a solid black square, the stave lines being type " rules," as evidenced by the fact that the pieces forming the lines are imperfectly joined. We give a reproduction of this very crude but interesting example of the earliest typographic music printing executed in England. De Worde must accordingly be given the credit of being the first English music printer from movable types. (Fig. 14.)

The plain chant in the Mainz (or Mentz) Psalter of 1490 was printed by Peter Schoeffer, an associate of Gutenberg, to whom we have already alluded as the inventor of printing from movable type. It is recorded that Schoeffer made the type for this edition, and the fact that his second son became a very clever engraver of punches for music type gives ground for believing that the elder Schoeffer may have used music type at an earlier date. Type from the punches cut by the son was used for a work published as early as 1512.

Apparently music printing from type became pretty general soon after the appearance of Schoeffer's edition of the Mainz Psalter, for there are records of music printing in various countries soon afterwards, notably in Italy, at Milan in 1496, and Brescia in 1497. There is, however, no definite evidence of their using movable type, and the credit for being the first to do this after Schoeffer is given to Ottaviano Petrucci, who established a music-printing press in Venice in

25

1498, and who about the year 1500 began producing
Mass books with the music printed in lozenge-shaped
notes. In 1513 he removed to Fossombrone, his

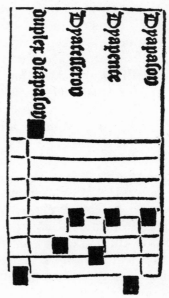

Fig. 14

EXAMPLE OF MUSIC IN HIGDEN'S " POLICHRONICON,"
PRINTED BY WYNKYN DE WORDE

native place; and Pope Leo X granted him a
monopoly for the use of music types.

The example we give (Fig. 15) shows that Petrucci's
work was beautifully regular compared with anything
that had been done before, but his method had the
drawback that it involved two printings—one for the
staves and the other for the notes.

Several printers in other countries either followed

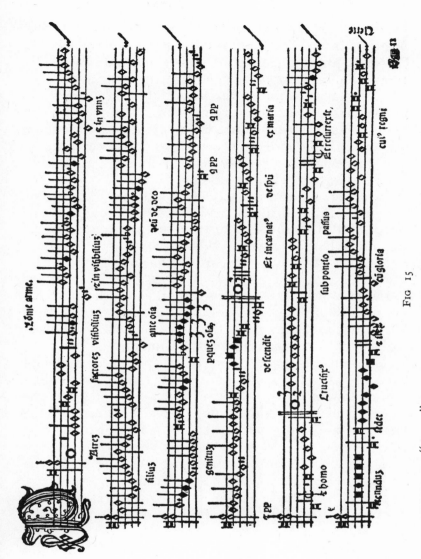

FIG 15

A PAGE OF A "MASS" BY PIERRE DE LA RUE. PRINTED BY OTTAVIANO DEI PETRUCCI

Petrucci's example or independently worked at music printing from type. In 1501, Nicholas Wollinck, at Cologne, printed plain-song music in that way. In 1506, similar work was done at Augsburg ; and, in 1507, Erhard Oeglin, of the latter city, executed work in which both the staves and notes were printed at one impression from music type. This was a distinct advance, the advantage of which was soon recognized, and thenceforward the system of printing the stave lines separately fell into disuse.

In 1525 (one authority says 1532), Briard, of Avignon, France, introduced notes with oval-shaped heads, but the squared lozenge shapes continued in use for a long time after this date.

Mathias Apiarius, of Strasburg and Berne, who published musical works by typographic printing between 1520 and 1553, was another of the pioneers of music printing. Examples of his work show very regular setting of the stave lines. He used lozenge-headed notes and a five-line stave.

The music characters engraved by Guillaume le Bé (1540–1592), at Venice, are very clearly cut. His work shows both the old lozenge-shaped notes and the newer ones with oval heads. He also joined up the quavers, and employed a six-line stave, also showing flats.

There are also records of music printing in Parma in 1526, Lyons in 1532, and Nuremburg in 1549.

Pierre Attaignat, at Paris, in 1529, was the first to print the words of songs under the notes. We give an example of his work. (Fig. 16.)

Although, as we have shown, some attempt was

made to do music printing in England as early as 1495, there is no record of anything further being done until 1530, when type similar to that of Petrucci's was employed, and the impressions made in two printings.

Richard Steele, in his monograph on music printing down to 1600, refers to Rastell, or his successor Gough, as having been the first to introduce into

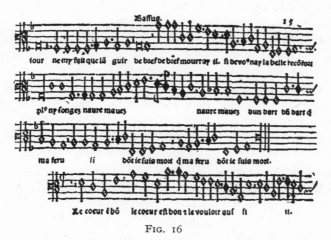

FIG. 16

MUSIC PRINTING OF PIERRE ATTAIGNAT, WHO WAS THE FIRST TO PRINT THE WORDS OF SONGS UNDER THE NOTES

England the system of printing music from type at one impression. A work done in this way was published by Gough in 1539. It is stated that the Gough type required about forty punches for its manufacture, whilst a full set of the later type of 1560 would require about seventy; and a full set in 1693 contained about 200. It is interesting to compare the growth in the number of characters in music type of that day with a later period of which there is a record. In 1794, for instance, it is stated that Caslon, the famous English typefounder, had in stock 220 punches for music type, and 298 matrices of all sorts, one of the sets containing seventy matrices. At the present day, a fount of music type consists of about 500 characters. The reason for this increase in the number of characters will be explained in a later chapter.

Those who wish to study early music printing from type characters will find plenty of opportunities in all the great libraries, such as the British Museum, the libraries of the Universities of Oxford and Cambridge, the libraries of English cathedrals, and in the great Continental libraries ; but, generally speaking, there is a sameness about most of the early typographic music printing. The face of the type does not vary much and the notes are closely set, whilst the printing is generally poor. The works printed are mostly for Church services ; indeed, the production of Church music has always afforded the greatest scope for music printing, and in the earliest days was the greatest incentive to its execution.

One of the earliest uses of typographic music in England was in the publication of the Litany, which was the first form of prayer to be translated in England at the Reformation. The English translation was first published, without musical notes, in the reign of Henry VIII, on 27th May, 1544. Three weeks later, another copy, with plain-song annexed, was printed in London by Grafton, who was one of the first to regularly engage in the business of music printing in England. In this copy, the priest's part is in black notes and that for the choir in red.

Grafton was originally a grocer, but went to Paris with Edward Whitchurch, about 1537, at the suggestion and by the aid of Thomas Cromwell, for the purpose of getting the Bible printed in English. When nearly completed, the Inquisition seized the printer whom Grafton and Whitchurch employed, and the two partners had to fly to England. They afterwards bought a number of the confiscated copies and completed the work in London. Thenceforward, Grafton seems to have fully engaged in the printing business and obtained from Henry VIII a patent for the printing of Bibles, and many editions with the Psalter appeared.

In 1550, Grafton printed Merbecke's *Booke of Common praier noted*. The musical part was done in movable type, the four stave lines being printed in red and the notes in black. Only four kinds of notes were used, and in his quaint directions the author says—

In this boke is contayned so much of the Order of Common Praier as is to be sunge in the Churches wherein are used only these iiii sortes of notes—

The first is a strene note, and is a breve. The second is a square note, and is a semybreve. The iii. is a prycke and is a mynymme. And when there is a prycke by the square note, that prycke is half as much as the note that goeth before it. The iiii. is a close and is only used at the end of a verse.

John Merbecke, the author of these delightfully simple instructions, was organist of St. George's Chapel Royal, Windsor, and some of his music is sung in our churches at the present day.

Merbecke, in addition to the change of the names of the time notes in conformity with the more modern notation, introduces two characters not usually found in the more ancient plain-song, namely, the dot and the pause.

There is an old Bible in the Blades' Library of the St. Bride's Institute, London, dated 1579, printed by Christopher Barker, which has in it some typographic music interspersed in the text of the Psalms. The notes are lozenge-shaped and are connected with the stave lines.

Up to 1690 or thereabouts, each note was a separate character in typographic music. The system of joining together the hooks of the quavers and semiquavers was introduced by a London music printer named John Heptinstall, who claimed the credit of being the first to introduce the " new tied note," which consisted of tying the quavers together with a thick line connecting the stems. The absence of this feature in typographic music had caused engraved music to be preferred for most of the instrumental music of the day. It was quite easy in the engraving to tie the notes together, and this was, in fact, done long before Heptinstall did it with type. The " new tied note " was afterwards improved upon by William Pearson, who was printing musical works a few years later than Heptinstall, and who printed John Playford's *Introduction to the skill of Musick*, which was published

32

in 1700. An earlier edition had been issued in 1687, printed by Charles Peregrine. We reproduce a page from each of these editions (Figs. 17, 18) showing the great improvement made in musical typography by Pearson. In the page from the 1700 edition, the " new tied note " will be seen, whilst the character of the notes approaches nearly the style of modern printing.

It may be thought curious that half the page is printed upside down, but the reason is that some of these early music books were designed to be used by two persons, each holding the book and facing each other.

John Playford has been credited with having introduced the " new tied note " in 1660 ; but as the year of his birth is 1623 and he died in 1693, this seems incredible, for, as we have shown, the first work in which the new style appears was published in 1700, though there may have been earlier editions in which the new system was used. His son Henry succeeded him and carried on the business, and published the 1700 edition, but he died in 1710. A younger brother, who died in 1686, was also in business as a music printer, and reprinted some of his father's works.

Heptinstall also introduced a further improvement, that of making the heads of the notes round instead of lozenge-shaped ; but, as we have already shown, this had been done by Briard, in France, in 1525 or 1532.

At Edinburgh, in 1615, Andro Hart printed *The CL Psalmes of David in Scottish Meter* from movable type. This shows that the art of typographic music

33

COUNTER-TEN. C *sol fa ut* Cliff *on the third Line.*

Sol la *mi* fa sol la fa sol   Sol la fa sol la *mi* fa fol

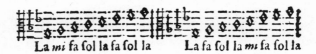

La *mi* fa sol la fa sol la   La fa sol la *mi* fa sol la

TENOR, C *sol fa ut* Cliff *on the fourth line.*

La fa sol la *mi* fa sol la   *Mi* fa sol la fa sol la *mi*

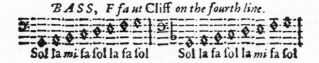

Fa sol la *mi* fa sol la fa   Fa fol la fa sol la *mi* fa

BASS, F *fa ut* Cliff *on the fourth line.*

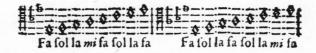

Sol la *mi* fa sol la fa sol   Sol la fa sol la *mi* fa sol

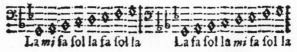

La *mi* fa sol la fa sol la   La fa sol la *mi* fa sol la

FIG. 17

A PAGE FROM JOHN PLAYFORD'S "INTRODUCTION TO THE
SKILL OF MUSICK" (1687 EDITION)

Short AYRES *or* SONGS *of* *Two Voices,*
Treble *and* Baſs, *for Beginners.*

A 2 *Voc.*   *TREBLE.*   *W. L.*

Ather   your Roſe-buds while you   may, old

Time is   ſtill   a   fly·-ing, and that ſame Flow'r that

ſmiles to   day,   to mor—row will be dy—ing.

FIG. 18

A PAGE FROM JOHN PLAYFORD'S "INTRODUCTION TO THE
SKILL OF MUSICK" (1700 EDITION)

35

printing had been introduced in Scotland at quite an early date.

Numerous music books were issued during the reigns of Elizabeth and James, but they were produced under a series of arbitrary and monopolizing patents. The first was granted in the seventeenth year of Elizabeth's reign (1575) to Tallis and Bird for twenty-one years. The two shared the post of honorary organist at the Chapel Royal, and they obtained the monopoly from Elizabeth for printing and selling music paper (English and foreign), the penalty for infringement being 40s. The monopoly does not seem to have been very valuable, as a petition in the Stationers' Register records that—

Bird & Tallys . . . have music bokes with notes which the complainants confess they wold not print nor be furnished to print though there were no privilege.

In 1577, Bird petitioned the Queen for a lease in reversion for twenty-one years of the value of £40, as he was fallen into debt and necessity. The licence for the printing of music had fallen, to their loss and hindrance, to the value of 200 marks at least. On the death of Tallis in 1585, the benefit of the monopoly became the sole property of Bird, who during the next few years was unusually active in composition. He collaborated with Bull and Orlando Gibbons in the collection of virginal music entitled *Parthenia*, published probably in 1611, and towards the end of his life was in better circumstances. He died in 1623. One of his earliest works was printed in 1575 by Thomas Vautrollier, and another in 1588 by Thomas Easte, who were his assignees under the patent.

36

From the reference above to *Parthenia*, it would appear that some of the music published by Tallis and Bird was printed from plates, as it is stated that *Parthenia* was the first music printed in England from engraved plates. This claim is contested by some authorities, who hold that Gibbons's *Fantasia of Three parts for Viols* has an earlier date. The exact year of publication is doubtful, 1609 and 1610 being variously given. The present chapter, however, does not concern plate-printed music, and we defer its consideration to our next chapter.

Another very early example of music printing is that which appears in a work entitled *The Noble Art of Venerie or Hunting*, by George Turberville, printed by Henry Bynnemann for Christopher Barker in 1575, a second edition being issued in 1611. This is a quarto book, and the music is a short passage for the hunting horn. Some authorities have stated that this is printed from a plate ; but Mr. F. Kidson, a well-known writer on early printed music, contends that it has been printed from a raised surface, probably a woodcut, as the work is freely adorned with wood engravings.

The style of type used in these early days of music printing can be studied in a book printed by Thomas Harper, *The Second Booke of Ayres*, by John Playford. A page of this work is here reproduced, and it illustrates the character of the type used. (Fig. 19.)

In the Blades' Library are several old Psalters, bearing dates from 1588 to 1640, in which there are portions of music from type interspersed amongst the text. The notes are all lozenge-shaped, and the

37

Er't thou more fairer then thou art, which lies not in the power of art,

or hadst thou in thine eyes more darts, then ever Cupid shot at hearts, yet if they were not

shot at me, I should not cast a thought on thee.

I'de rather marry a disease,
Then court the thing I cannot please ;
She that would cherrish my desires
Must court my flames with equall fires :
What pleasure is there in a kisse
To him that doubts the heart's not his ?

I love thee not because thou art faire,
Softer then downe, smoother then ayre ;
Not for the Cupids that lye
In either corner of thine eye :
Would you then know what it might be ?
'Tis I love you, 'cause you love me.

FIG. 19

A PAGE FROM "THE SECOND BOOK OF AYRES," PRINTED
FROM MOVABLE TYPE BY THOMAS HARPER IN 1652

staves are very small, being in some cases not more than $\frac{1}{4}$ in. high.

A good example is *The Whole Booke of Psalmes, printed for the Allignes of Richard Day.* This is dated 1588. We give a reproduction of the page showing a metrical version of " The Lorde's Prayer " (Fig. 20) and also the hymn "Veni Creator " (Fig. 21).

Another interesting example is *The whole Booke o, Psalmes,* by T. Sternhold and John Hopkins, published in 1636. We reproduce a portion of the page on which appears the psalm " Regard O Lord." The type and staves are of a bolder character. (Fig. 22.)

In this Library are also several old musical instruction books, which contain interesting examples of typographically-printed music. *The Principles of Musik,* by Charles Butler (1636), is the earliest. We reproduce a portion showing its quaint character. (Fig. 23.) Another is dated 1678, entitled *Compendium of Practical Music,* by Christopher Simpson. This work contains one page which is printed from a crudely engraved plate, and the rest are from type. We reproduce specimens of both kinds. (Figs. 24, 25.)

Another interesting specimen of typographically-printed music is *Orpheus Britannicus : Collection of all the Choicest Songs,* by Henry Purcell, dated 1706, and it is noteworthy by reason of the notes approaching more the modern style, having oval-shaped heads. The staves are $\frac{3}{8}$ in. high, and there are a number of large folio pages of music. (Fig. 26.)

There are also some old Dutch and French Psalters and Bibles in the same Library bearing dates 1643,

4—(2370

FIG. 20

A PAGE FROM "THE WHOLE BOOKE OF PSALMES," PRINTED BY RICHARD DAY (1588 EDITION)

1734, 1771, and 1773, all having music amongst the text, lozenge-shaped notes being used. Of another style are two service books : *Ceremoniale Episcoporum*, published in Rome, 1651, with square notes in black on staves printed in red ; and *Processionarium* (Rome, 1754), also printed in black notes with red staves

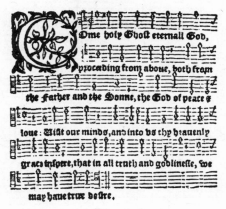

FIG. 21

A PAGE FROM "THE WHOLE BOOKE OF PSALMES" (STERNHOLD AND HOPKINS). PUBLISHED 1588. PRINTED BY RICHARD DAY

but some of the notes are lozenge-shaped. The type is poor and badly aligned.

Coming down to a later date (1818), there are two Testaments printed in Dutch bearing the imprint of Joh. Enschede en Zonen, of Haarlem, a very old firm of typefounders and printers still flourishing in that city. They still possess some of the old music type, which the author has inspected in their private

41

museum ; and in recent years the firm have used the old founts for setting up ornamental borders.

The staves in these old Testaments are very close

FIG. 22

A PAGE FROM "THE WHOLE BOOKE OF PSALMES," (STERNHOLD AND HOPKINS). PUBLISHED IN 1636

ruled, being only about $\frac{1}{8}$ in. high. The notes have lozenge-shaped heads.

The example (Fig. 27) which we give of a page of Church music, printed in 1843 by Jas. Brydone, Edinburgh, illustrates very well the style of music

42

printing done at that time. The printer was grand-father of the founder of the firm of Lowe & Brydone, the well-known London music printers of the present day.

A good deal of information concerning the progress of music typography in England can be gleaned from T. B. Reed's *History of Old English Letter Foundries*, and most interesting are the notes concerning Peter Walpergen, a Dutch punch-cutter, who settled down

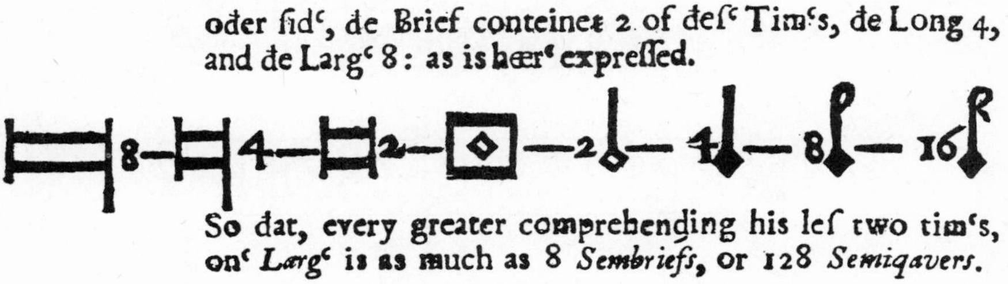

oder ſidᶜ, de Brief conteinet 2 of deſᶜ Timᶜs, de Long 4, and de Largᶜ 8 : as is hæᵉrᶜ expreſſed.

So dat, every greater comprehending his leſ two timᶜs, onᶜ *Largᶜ* is as much as 8 *Sembriefs*, or 128 *Semiqavers*.

FIG. 23

PORTION OF A PAGE FROM "THE PRINCIPLES OF MUSIK," BY CHARLES BUTLER (1636)

in Oxford about 1672. He cut a set of music punches somewhere about the year 1695, and the punches and matrices are still preserved by the University Press, Oxford, to which they were presented by Bishop Fell, who was evidently a patron of typefounders and printers. He had a large collection of punches, matrices, and tools for making the same, all of which he presented to the University. Walpergen's music punches numbered seventy, and they were apparently bought by Bishop Fell at the time of the punch-cutter's death. There is extant an inventory of his goods, showing that sixty-three music punches were

43

valued at 5s. the lot, other punches and matrices being marked at what seems now an absurdly low figure.

In Reed's book a specimen of music printing is given, which has been set up from type cast from

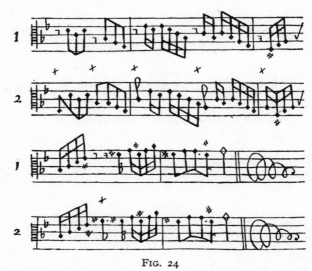

FIG. 24

PAGE FROM "A COMPENDIUM OF MUSICK," BY CHRISTOPHER
SIMPSON (1678)

Walpergen's original matrices. The notes have curious pear-shaped heads, and the characters are wonderfully clean and sharply cut, whilst the stave lines join up very neatly. When presented by Bishop Fell, the punches were described as new, which may account for this sharpness of the type.

It is recorded that, in 1794, an inventory of punches and matrices in possession of the University included 220 punches for music type, and two lots of matrices to the number of 228 and 70 respectively.

Some of the types possessed by the University are

Rudiments of Song. 25

Tripla *of three* Minims *to a* Mea*ſure,*

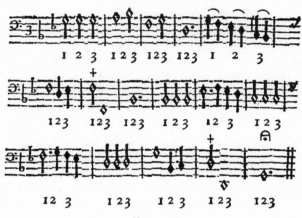

FIG. 25

TYPE SET PAGE FROM " A COMPENDIUM OF MUSICK," BY CHRISTOPHER SIMPSON (1678)

thought to be from Walpergen's punches, whilst others are stated to be from an unknown source (as in the example we have given, Fig. 7, *ante*). From certain documentary evidence, these are thought to be of Dutch origin.

From Reed's interesting work we take the following

particulars concerning various old English founders of music type—

John Day, some time about the year 1582, cut a new fount of music type for his editions of the metrical psalter. The notes were chiefly lozenge shape and hollow (white), differing from those of Grafton shown in Merbecke's *Booke of Common Praier*, which are mostly square and solid (black). Day says, in a book printed in 1582, that he " caused a new

Charmes, 'tis Heav'n, 'tis Heav'n to lye with-in- - - - - her Armes; while I ſtand gazing on her

FIG. 26

EXAMPLE OF MUSIC IN " ORPHEUS BRITANNICA," BY HENRY PURCELL (1706)

print of notes to be made with letters to be joined to every note, whereby thou mayest know how to call every note by its right name."

Joseph Moxon, an old typefounder of about this period, who published a book entitled *Mechanik Exercises*, describes what he terms a " joynt flat gauge " for polishing the faces of punches before hardening and before striking into the copper.

Robert Andrews succeeded Moxon, probably about the year 1683, and a list of music matrices in his foundry, in 1706, included 54 of two-line Great Primer, 44 of Paragon square head, 61 of large old square

46

head, and 155 sundry, these being the descriptions given in the inventory.

James Grover (1675) was supposed to have in his

FIG. 27

EXAMPLE OF MUSIC PRINTED BY JAMES BRYDONE,
EDINBURGH (1843)

foundry the founts belonging to Wynkyn de Worde. A list of his matrices includes 176 for Great Primer music type.

Robert Mitchell, who succeeded Godfrey Head in

47

1685, had some music matrices. His foundry was purchased in 1739 by William Caslon and John James, who divided the contents between them.

In an inventory of the Caslon Foundry of about the year 1766, there is mentioned some matrices of round head music notes cut by Caslon II, who died in 1778.

Dr. Fry, of Bristol, had a foundry in 1764, and in a specimen book of his types, published in 1824, are music types described as "Large Plein Chant, small ditto, and Psalm."

Leaving the account of further progress in typographic music at this point, we deal next with engraved or stamped music, in order to maintain the chronological sequence of our record.

CHAPTER III

THE term "engraving" is applied indiscriminately by writers on early music printing, and even in regard to modern music, whether the music plates are punched or wholly engraved. As we shall show in later chapters, all music plates are at least partially engraved, but for the present we are dealing with music which was wholly engraved. This is really the finest kind of music engraving, and yielded the most beautiful results even in the very earliest times. The engravers were usually men who were highly skilled in pictorial or commercial engraving and possessed a high degree of craftsmanship.

Tracing the origin and progress of this form of music engraving, we find it recorded that Pierre Hautin, a French copperplate engraver (some describe him as a typefounder), in 1525, cut punches for lozenge-shaped musical notes, combining both note and stave, and that these punches were used for stamping into metal plates. If this statement were well authenticated, this would be the foundation of the method of music engraving used to-day, and to France would belong the honour of the invention.

The year 1586 is, however, generally given as the earliest date of the introduction of engraved music. In that year, a collection of canzonets, engraved by

49

Martin van Buyten, was published by Simone Verovio in Rome. The method, proving popular, was soon adopted in England, France, Germany, and the Netherlands.

Copperplate engraving originated from *niello* engraving, a process by which a design engraved intaglio on silver or other metallic articles was filled in with a black composition so as to show up the engraving. Impressions were taken from these engravings before filling in, and this probably suggested the art of engraving on metal for printing purposes; and the invention in this respect is ascribed to Finiguerra, the Florentine goldsmith, about 1452. It rapidly progressed as a means for printing pictures and text, and from 1500 and onward the process was extensively used.

Mr. F. Kidson (in Grove's *Dictionary of Music*) remarks—

While the arts of engraving and etching for pictorial purposes had attained a high degree of perfection during the seventeenth century, it is singular that so obvious a method, and so superior a one to that where the clumsy music typography of the day was employed, should have been so seldom used.

England was evidently early in the field of the application of engraving to music printing, for it is stated that, in 1598, Thomas Morley had brought the art of engraving music on copperplates, and printing from them, to the highest degree of perfection possible in those days. A patent monopoly was granted to him for it.

In the reign of James I, and under date 1611, a musical work entitled *Parthenia* was published, and

50

the work was described as "entirely engraven on copperplates." This book is often quoted as the first book printed in England from plates, but the statement is challenged by reference to Gibbons's *Fantasia of Three Parts for Viols.* The date of this is variously fixed at 1609 and 1610, but the actual year is uncertain, and some authorities have fixed it between 1614 and 1639. The work is said to be "cut in copper, the like not before extant." Both *Parthenia* and *Fantasia* were reprinted several times from the same plates.

By about the year 1680 plate-engraved music had become pretty general in England. There is a statement published that in 1683, Thomas Cross began to engrave music, and that he soon made a revolution in English music publishing. Plate-printed music certainly became much more in evidence from this date onward, and after 1700 it was the rule rather than the exception to issue music from plates.

Thomas Cross was practically the inventor of sheet music. His name first appears in 1683 on Purcell's *Sonatas of III Parts.* It is there given as "Thos. Cross, junior, sculp." He so signed himself during the lifetime of his father, who was also an engraver, though there is no evidence that he engraved music. Between 1683 and 1732 Cross appears to have had nearly the whole of the music engraving trade in his hands, working for composers as well as publishers. His work was particularly neat and cleanly cut on copper, in a bold and free style, his lettering being very flowing. His later engraving is not so fine and minute as the earlier, but is quite clear and legible.

51

About the year 1697, he began engraving the issue of single songs. All vocal music prior to this period had to be purchased in collections chiefly printed from type. Instrumental music had been engraved in separate pieces to a small extent ; in fact, nearly all engraved music down to this time was instrumental.

There are indications that Cross (except in his very early work) did much of his engraving on either zinc or pewter, and probably used in some cases the etching needle and acid. Copper was expensive for such ephemeral productions as Cross issued, and which had to be sold at a cheap rate. The single songs were printed on a half sheet of paper, and must have come forth in enormous numbers. At the foot of most of the sheets the engraver's imprint reads : " Exactly engraved by T. Cross."

About 1720, or a little later, Cross had a serious rival in the publication of sheet songs. John Walsh commenced to issue them in similar form, but from plates produced by punching the notes and lettering in the pewter. This caused Cross to engrave on one of his sheets : " Beware of ye nonsensical puncht ones.—Cross, Sculp."

Cross kept a music shop in Katherine Wheel Court, Snow Hill, " near Holborn Conduit," and afterwards " near the Pound, Clerkenwell."

About this time the Dutch appear to have introduced a method of softening copper, so that the notes could be readily stamped on the plate. John Walsh and John Hare are stated to have introduced the process into England about 1710, but probably the date may be a few years earlier ; and it hardly seems

52

probable that these engravers employed the process so early, seeing that they did not put it to effective use until 1720, when they set out to compete with Cross.

A feature of the engraved music of that day, distinguishing it from typographic music, was that the quavers and semiquavers were joined in groups as in the manuscript music of the same period. In typographic music, before the introduction of the " tied note," the quavers were separate.

The earliest example of engraved music in France seems to be dated about 1675, when the music of " Phaeton," the opera of Lulli, was engraved by H. de Baussen. The notes are of the lozenge form of the old typography. We here reproduce a portion of this music (Fig. 28), and for comparison we give an example (Fig. 29) engraved by Mdlle. Roussel (the first woman music engraver of whom there is any record) in 1720. The example engraved by Madame Leroy in 1800 is also interesting. (Fig. 30.)

The art of music engraving was introduced at a very early date into America, for it is recorded that the first music printed in that country was done in 1690 from engraved plates. Probably the plates were imported from England, for the earliest recorded music engraving actually done in America is that for a collection of Church music published by Josiah Flagg in 1764. It is interesting to note that the plates were engraved by Paul Revere, the hero of Longfellow's poem, " Paul Revere's Ride."

In the Blades' Library there are some early examples of engraved music. For instance, *A*

Fig. 28

EXAMPLE OF MUSIC IN THE OPERA OF "PHAETON," BY LULLI, ENGRAVED BY H. BAUSSEN (1675)

Fig. 29

EXAMPLE OF MUSIC ENGRAVED BY MDLLE. LOUISE ROUSSEL (1720)

Fig. 30

EXAMPLE OF MUSIC ENGRAVED BY MADAME LEROY (1800)

Treatise of the Natural Grounds and Principles of Harmony, by William Holder, D.D., published in London in 1694. This contains some music printed from copper-plates.

Another early work is *Observations on Florid Song*, by Pier Francesco Tosi, translated into English by Galliard, and published in London in 1742. The

FIG. 31

EXAMPLE FROM "OBSERVATIONS ON FLORID SONG"
(1742)

music is fairly well engraved, and is printed direct from the plates. (Fig. 31.)

A further specimen of this period is *A New Musical Grammar , or, The Harmonical Spectator*, by William Tansur, London, 1746. The example we give (Fig. 32) shows how crudely the music is engraved. It is so very amateurish that one might imagine the author had engraved the plates himself.

By about the beginning of the eighteenth century, music printing from type had declined very considerably. The reason probably was that musical composition had become more elaborate and the old

FIG. 32

A PAGE FROM " A NEW MUSICAL GRAMMAR (1746)

movable type was found inadequate to represent it. Copperplate engraving, which was then flourishing and largely used, was, therefore, naturally adopted. This method was, however, found expensive, so that it became in a measure superseded by the method of punching the notes on pewter plates. This process did not become common until the middle of the eighteenth century. The year 1710 is given as the date of its introduction into England, and, as already stated, Walsh and Hare are mentioned as having introduced it, but it seems likely that the actual date was a few years earlier. John Walsh published a work printed from pewter plates in October, 1724 ; and its author, Dr. Croft, speaks of the production as by a new and improved method of printing. It is said that the first collection of Church music punched on pewter plates was Dr. Croft's *Musica Sacra.*

In the Blades' Library there is a book entitled *The Merry Musician, A Cure for Spleen, printed for and sold by I. Walsh, Music Printer and Instrument Maker to His Majesty.* The music is punched and printed from the original plates, the work being rather crude. We give a reproduction of one of the pages. (Fig. 33.) The date of publication is not given, which may be explained by the statement of writer on early printed music that " prior to the eighteenth century, Playford and the earlier printers honestly gave the year of issue, but wily John Walsh discovered that women and music should never be dated."

If Walsh did, in fact, introduce punched music into England, it is most probable that he imported

A Cure for the Spleen.

The VICAR of BRAY.

In Charles the Second's Golden Days, when

Loyalty no harm meant, A furious high Church

Man I was, and fo I gaind preferment;

Un_to my Flock I daily preach'd, Kings are by

God appointed, and Damn'd are thofe who

.dare refift, or touch the Lord's Anointed.

And this is Law I will maintain un_to my

Dying Day Sir, That whatfoever King fhall

Reign, I will be Vicar of Bray Sir.

FIG. 33

A PAGE FROM " THE MERRY MUSICIAN " (1785)

it from France, where, as already stated at the opening of this chapter, it was invented in 1525 by Hautin. A somewhat contradictory statement of one authority is that, soon after 1730, punches were used for stamping the heads of notes on the plates.

The idea of the process undoubtedly originated from the practice of the typefounders, who cut the letters on steel punches and then stamped them into copper. This art is much older than music engraving, and it would be an obvious method for saving the tedious practise of completely engraving the plate.

Other metals besides pewter were tried for punching-on. There is a statement extant that towards the close of the seventeenth century the Dutch, who excelled in music punching as well as in engraving it, found a way of softening copper for this purpose. It is also recorded that Dr. Crysander used zinc for his beautiful edition of Handel's works.

It is stated that pewter plates were at first regarded as a failure for music punching, and that it was not till the end of the eighteenth century that their employment became really successful.

Engraved music certainly held its own for some years after the introduction of punching, and after 1700 it was the rule rather than the exception to issue music from engraved plates. There are records of excellent work of this kind being produced in Paris in 1725, and in Vienna in 1730. Handel's " Suites " were engraved by Cluer in 1720, and J. C. Smith's " Suites " about the same period. Bach's *Clavier Uebung* was engraved by the composer himself.

Gradually, however, the engraved plate was superseded by the stamped pewter plate, mainly, no doubt, on account of the cheapness of the latter and through the facility with which corrections could be made.

In an article on " Music Printing " in the' *Printing Times and Lithographer*, 1875 (p. 208), the author says—

The great improvement made in this art in England is due to one Phillips, who produced some fine specimens, deriving his principles from Fortier, a French watchmaker of some celebrity as well as a stamper of music plates.

The date of Phillips's work is not given ; but another authority says that at the end of the eighteenth century, a London engraver greatly improved the method, especially improving the punches. Possibly this engraver was Phillips.

The three principal engravers of the eighteenth century were William Smith (working about 1730 to 1762), and John Phillips and his wife Sarah (1750–1763). In Scotland, at Edinburgh, Richard Cooper worked from about 1725 to 1764. He was the first who engraved music in Scotland, his earliest work being a small oblong volume of music which Allan Ramsay issued, about 1725, as a companion to his *Tea Table Miscellany*. This work is now so scarce, that it is doubtful if more than one perfect copy exists. Its title is *Musick for Allan Ramsay's Collection of Scot's Songs, set by Alexander Stuart . . . engraved by R. Cooper*. Besides engraving music, Cooper engraved some very fine portraits.

L. T. Phinn and James Read were a little later ; while James Johnson, from 1722 to 1811, monopolized

Example of Arpeggios.

FIG. 34

PAGE FROM "A MUSICAL VADE MECUM" (1820)

the whole of the Scottish trade. In Dublin, Manwaring and the Neal family worked about the middle of the eighteenth century.

There is a list of English engraved music books before 1700 given in the article by Mr. F. Kidson in Grove's *Dictionary of Music*.

Anyone who wishes to examine some of the old punched music may do so in a couple of works in the Blades' Library. One is *A Musical Vade Mecum*, by R. W. Keith, London. The date is not given on the title-page, but a review quoted at the end shows that it was published in 1820. This work is interesting because the whole of the explanatory text and music is punched, and the pages show the plate marks, indicating that they were printed direct from the plates in the copperplate press. The music is very well done, and the lettering is not bad considering the methods employed. We reproduce an example of the work. (Fig. 34.) The other work is *The Psalms and Hymns used at the Asylum or House of Refuge for Female Orphans* (the institution now popularly known as the Foundling Hospital). No date is printed on it, but the date 1845 is written on the title-page. The punching and printing is in the same manner as the preceding work.

CHAPTER IV

APPLICATION OF LITHOGRAPHY TO MUSIC PRINTING

THE important part played by lithography almost from the date of its invention down to the present time deserves special mention, for it is not too much to say that but for this method the printing of music would have remained as crude, slow, and costly as the processes we have indicated in the previous chapters.

The art of lithography was discovered in 1796 by Alois Senefelder, son of Peter Senefelder, a Court actor of Munich. Alois became a dramatic author and actor himself, and it was in seeking for a method of printing his pieces that he was induced to make experiments which led to the invention of lithography.

At first, Senefelder tried engraving on copper and zinc, but these materials being expensive and troublesome to polish, the idea occurred to him of using a kind of limestone which he was using as a slab for mixing his inks upon.

His first idea was to etch the stone in the same way he had been doing on metal, but he eventually found that it was easier to print from the surface of the stone. Drawing or writing was done direct on it, using an ink which contained grease or wax ; and by keeping the bare parts of the stone moistened with gum and water, a roller charged with greasy printing ink could be passed over it. This had the effect of depositing ink on the lines of the design without the bare parts receiving any, as the ink was repelled by the moisture on the stone. The principle of the method was that greasy ink (that forming the design) repelled moisture, whilst the moisture, in turn, repelled the greasy ink applied by the rollers, the ink being attracted only by the greasy ink of the design, because there was no moisture there to repel it. By laying a sheet of paper on the inked stone and applying pressure, prints were taken from the design. The stone was moistened after each impression, re-inked, and a further print taken. This is essentially the method of lithography still practised at the present day, the only important modifications made being the use of zinc or aluminium plates, with better mechanical means of printing them.

Senefelder disclaims the merit of originality of thought in the conception of the idea. He says—

I remember that as a child of five or six I had seen a music printery in Frankfurt or Mainz, where the notes were etched in black slate stone. I had played with the broken stones which lay in a heap near our house.

It is an interesting fact that music printing thus gave rise to the idea of lithography, and that the first application of it was to the purpose of printing music.

In his autobiographical work, *The Invention of Lithography*, Senefelder says—

Some very badly printed music that I bought at Ingoldstadt awakened the idea that with my new printing process I would furnish much better work.

64

He went with his idea to Herr Gleissner, the Court
musician, who encouraged him to try to print some
music ; and Senefelder says—

My printing succeeded absolutely. Gleissner marvelled at the
swiftness and beauty of the impressions, and, knowing my penni-
less condition, he offered of his own free will to pay for a small
printery.

Senefelder further says—

Herr Gleissner composed twelve songs with clavier accompani-
ment. I wrote them rapidly on stone, and made one hundred and
twenty impressions with the aid of a day labourer.

Many other orders followed, and Senefelder says—

I gained so much happy hope, that I thought myself richer
than Croesus.

Weber, the composer, who was intimately acquainted
with Senefelder, entirely forsook his musical studies
for a time to assist the latter in his efforts, and
Weber's " Opus No. 2 " was printed by lithography
in 1799. This was one of the first important pieces
of music printed by lithography.

Gleissner supported Senefelder in developing his
invention, and in 1800 a full description of the process was deposited in the archives of the English
Patent Office. It was intended to open a business
in London to print and publish music, and eventually
Senefelder came over to establish the business, stay-
ing here seven months. He trained one Philip Andre
to work the process, and left him in charge of the
business. Andre lost heavily on the transaction, and
Senefelder gained nothing by it. What happened to
the London business is not recorded, but Andre went
to France and Austria to exploit the process. At a

65

later date, however, lithography was introduced into England in a more practical way by Ackermann and, after that, was rapidly developed. The year 1830 is given as the date of the introduction of lithography into England.

Apparently it was soon discovered that it was possible to transfer from the punched music plates to the lithographic stone instead of drawing direct thereon or on transfer paper. *Jullien's Album*, 1847, a copy of which is in the Blades' Library, is a good example of such work, the music and words being lithographed together. It is printed by Hanhart, one of the earliest established London lithographers. (Fig. 35.)

The cylinder power press for lithographic printing was introduced about 1850, and this gave a great impetus to the production of music by lithography.

It is stated by one authority that lithography was not used for music printing in France until about 1855, but another writer says that about 1850 lithography by transfer was introduced into that country. This may refer to transfers pulled from engraved plates or to the process sometimes called autography, in which the music is drawn on transfer paper. A good example of autographed music is contained in *Les Livres Rares*, printed in Rennes in 1856 by the firm of Oberthur, which still flourishes there. A copy of this book is in the Blades' Library.

One of the earliest firms to engage in the printing and publication of lithographic music in this country is that of Augener & Co., now one of the largest music printing and publishing houses in this country. It

F_IG_. 35

REPRODUCTION OF LITHOGRAPHED MUSIC FROM JULLIEN'S ALBUM (1847)

was founded in 1853 by Mr. George Augener at 86 Newgate Street, London, E.C. Elsewhere we have noted that the firm bought the business of Gustav Scheurmann, who, in 1856, had invented a system of double printing of music, which consisted of printing the staves and notes separately from movable type, but the process never came to any success ; and Messrs. Augener have, with this slight exception, consistently adhered to the lithographic printing of engraved music, leaving typographic music to those who have specialized in that line.

The further developments of lithographic music to the present day are dealt with in a later chapter.

CHAPTER V

REVIVAL OF TYPOGRAPHIC MUSIC PRINTING

IT will be seen from the foregoing chapter that as engraved and lithographic music improved in quality, the older process of typographic music printing degenerated and fell into desuetude, but towards the end of the eighteenth century, attempts began to be made to revive this style of printing.

For instance, in 1765, Henry Fougt, a German engraver, who had a business in London, first in St. Martin's Lane and afterwards at Salisbury Court, Fleet Street, proposed a method for which he took out a patent in 1767. The specification may be seen in the Patent Office, numbered 888 in that year. His claim is for " certain new and curious types by me invented for the printing of music as neatly and as well in every respect as hath been usually done by engraving." He refers to the similarity of his characters to the " choral types " of the old music, but points out that in the latter the whole figure of the note with the five lines cast with it had to be used, the piece of type being, therefore, the full length of the stave. Fougt's method was to divide the figure of the note, with its tail or stem, and the five lines of the stave both in the length and height of every row, so that every note is divided into five separate pieces of type. Although the number of characters is augmented five times, there would, he claims, be

69

an advantage gained. The inventor says he got his idea from the floral and ornamental type, which is thus built up of several pieces. He describes how he works out his method by using squared tracing paper laid over sheets of printed music, selecting the portions of the notes or signs which come within the squares. Accompanying the specification is a lithographed representation of the characters he proposes to use, numbering 166 in all. We give an illustration which shows that the characters are very similar to the elements at present used in music founts. (Fig. 36.)

It is said that Fougt was the only printer in his day who produced any good music work. He submitted specimens to the Society of Arts and obtained a resolution from that body to the effect that " his method of printing was superior to any that had been used before in Great Britain, and that it could be performed much cheaper." He was the pioneer of cheap music, for he sold his sheet music at " one penny per page or 18 for a shilling." His method was evidently not a success financially, for it is recorded that he failed because those who punched on pewter plates copied his works and were able to undersell him. This seems hardly likely, as their average price was sixpence per sheet. He returned to his native land, after selling his patent to one Falconer, who is described as a disappointed harpsichord maker. History does not record whether the latter made any better success in music printing, though he continued to issue sheet songs in similar style and at an equally low price.

70

FIG. 36

DIAGRAM IN FOUGT'S PATENT (1767)

A more fortunate inventor of music type was Breitkopf, a printer of Leipzig, who, in 1755 (one authority says 1750), perfected a system by which a number of small characters forming portions of the notes or staves were cast to a uniform measure so as to justify when set up. The closeness of dates makes one wonder whether his fellow-countryman, Fougt, whose patent was not taken out till twelve years later, cribbed the idea and brought it over to England. Breitkopf issued a specimen sheet in 1764, and Fougt's method is first heard of in 1765. The Breitkopf specimen book illustrates the " lay " of a pair of printer's cases, showing as many as 238 characters. Breitkopf also issued type for plain chant music. He was the founder (in 1719) of the house of Breitkopf & Hartel, one of the largest music printing firms in Germany at the present day. His partner, Hartel, on coming into the business, introduced the system of engraving on pewter plates, to which in 1805 he added a lithographic department, with the co-operation of Senefelder.

Breitkopf's method was the foundation of the present-day systems of typographic music printing, and practically no important change has been made since, except in the design and cut of the characters and the addition of useful sorts.

The British typefounders and those of other countries began to introduce better cut founts of music type about the same time as Breitkopf put his founts on the market, probably deriving some of their ideas from his work ; and with better type available, letterpress printers were encouraged to turn their attention to this kind of printing. We have already traced the music type of the old typefounders down to 1794, the date of the Oxford University Press inventory. After that, until well into the beginning of the nineteenth century, there is an interregnum in which nothing notable in typographic music printing is recorded.

Hugh Hughes, in 1824, in his *Dictionary of Printing*, shows a specimen of music typography, observing that " the English music types have never to my knowledge undergone any improvement till within a few years, when Mr. Hughes cut two new founts (Nonpareil and Pearl) which are looked upon as the best we have." Apparently the Mr. Hughes referred to was a typefounder, not the author himself.

It does not seem possible to trace the date at which the present-day British typefounders started casting music type. We have already quoted in Chapter II a statement that Caslon, the oldest English typefounder, whose house has a continuous history down to the present time, had a stock of 220 punches in 1794, but the firm do not now cast any music type.

Miller & Richard, of Edinburgh, another very old-established type foundry, say they cannot give the exact date when they commenced casting music type, but they know they have been casting it for over sixty years.

We subsequently show that Mr. Alfred Novello had a special fount cut by the Soho Type Foundry in 1853, and it is indicated that he had already in his possession founts which he had purchased when he started as a printer in 1847.

Messrs. P. M. Shanks & Sons (formerly known as the Patent Type Founding Co.) issued a sample sheet of music type in 1863, but how long they were casting music type before that date the present members of the firm are unable to say.

Messrs. V. & J. Figgins (now R. H. Stevens & Co.) are a very old-established typefounding house, and one of their specimen sheets is preserved in the Blades' Library, but is not dated. We are not able to trace how early the firm were casting music type.

We are unaware of any other English typefounders who have laid themselves out for casting music type.

From the fact that Messrs. Clowes & Sons were casting their own type early in the nineteenth century, it may be assumed that music type at that time was not easily purchasable, but that the typefounders began to meet the demand which arose about 1850 when the Novello's commenced to popularize cheap music.

William Clowes & Sons, the well-known London printers, are probably the oldest existing English typographic music printers. The house was founded in 1803, and they were producing type-printed music very early in the nineteenth century. An article in the *Quarterly Review* for December, 1839, described their typefoundry of that day. They had a set of punches cut for casting their own music type, and it is recorded that their fount was reckoned a very fine one. They are still casting music type, though they have also purchased founts from the regular typefounders. They were one of the earliest firms to adopt the plaster process of stereotyping, and applied

74

it to making plates from the pages of type-set music, so as to avoid subjecting the type to the wear and tear of printing. At the present day, however, stereotyping has been superseded for this purpose by electrotyping, and all the music plates used by the firm are now produced by the latter process. The original type is never printed from.

This firm have printed *Hymns Ancient and Modern* from the original issue in 1861 down to the present

FIG. 37

SPECIMEN OF MUSIC IN PLAIN-SONG AND MODERN NOTATION

day, and have lately printed a large supplement. They have also produced the *Hymnal Companion, The Children's Hymn Book, Chope's Carols, Purcell's Songs, The Music Portfolio,* and many other musical works which have run into large editions.

In the Music Edition of *Hymns Ancient and Modern,* the music of the very old hymns is given in plain-song as well as in the modern notation, a special fount of type having been cut for it. We here give a small example, kindly furnished by Messrs. Clowes, showing this. (Fig. 37.)

An interesting specimen of this firm's work is the miniature edition of *Hymns Ancient and Modern*, the pages of a larger edition having been reduced by the photo-zinco process.

The firm also do lithographed music from punched plates, but the largest volume of music printing done by them is by the typographic method.

It is probably largely due to the firm of Novello that typographic music was revived and became popular. The history of this house is extremely interesting, and the important part it has played in the dissemination of cheap music deserves to be specially recorded.

Vincent Novello was a professor of music of Italian parentage, and he was led to enter into the music publishing business owing to the difficulties he met with in publishing one of his own works. He had to incur the expense himself for engraving and printing this work, as no publisher could be found to undertake it, and this venture was the foundation of a music publishing house which has become world-famous.

In 1847, Alfred Novello, son of the founder of the business, began as a printer ; and in a circular issued by him in that year, he informs his friends and patrons that he " has latterly organized a printing house for the production of works of typography in general, and more especially such as require movable music types." Then follow specimens of five founts of music type which he states he had added to his already ample stock. The punches for two of these founts— the Pearl-Nonpareil and the Gem Gregorian—had been cut expressly and at considerable cost for his own use, and were remarkable for their boldness and clearness. Soon afterwards, the "Gem," a fount used at the present time for the octavo editions, was designed, the work of cutting the punches being entrusted to Mr. Palmer, of the Soho Type Foundry. This fount was intended to be an improvement on the music types then in use, and no pains nor expense were spared to make it so. Experience had shown that new combinations and characters could be used with advantage, and many of these were cut for the new fount. The work being of a special character, and extremely difficult and expensive in its execution, took about six years to complete, and it was not until 1853–4 that the first fount was delivered to the Novello printing house.

A specimen of Gregorian type, also cut specially for the firm, is shown on the circular to which we have referred. All the types are beautifully cut and well printed, showing that typographic music at that date had attained a high degree of perfection.

Respecting one of the founts shown in the circular, Mr. Novello says—

The matrices have been cut at considerable cost, and great varieties of "sorts" enables printers to place headed notes of different sizes on the same staff, an advantage peculiar to this fount.

PART II

TECHNICAL DETAILS OF MUSIC
ENGRAVING AND PRINTING

CHAPTER VI

PRODUCTION OF ENGRAVED MUSIC— THE PEWTER PLATES

THE term " engraving " is here used in the sense in which it is usually understood in connection with the production of music plates.   The process, as we have already indicated, is a combination of punching and engraving on pewter or, as they are sometimes called, " tin " plates.

Though, as stated in the introductory chapters, zinc and soft copper have been tried for music engraving, these metals were not found satisfactory for several reasons.   Zinc appears promising because of its cheapness compared with pewter, but it has its disadvantages.   The punches are neither cut nor tempered for punching on such a relatively hard metal and, not being strong enough, would soon be broken or battered.   Greater force being required to strike the punch to the proper depth, it would not be easy for the workman used to pewter to regulate the strength of the blow to suit zinc or copper.

The operation of the engraving tools on zinc and copper would also be difficult for a man used to pewter, as the graver has a tendency to slip.   It might be urged that a man could get accustomed to the use of other metals, but, even so, there would be the fact that it would be more difficult to make corrections on zinc ; and, moreover, this metal does not lend itself so readily to being scraped, which we shall show to be an important feature of the work. There is also the objection that zinc plates are liable to become oxidized if not cleaned and stored away very carefully. Once pitted from this cause, they could not be used for a fresh printing, unless much time was expended in burnishing and scraping away such pitting, thus adding to the cost.

It might be thought that as the work of music engraving is similar to copperplate engraving, and as the transfers are pulled from the same presses as are used for the latter, copper would be a better metal for standing the wear and tear of printing ; but most of the objections we have urged against the use of zinc, apply equally to copper. Besides, the much higher cost of the metal would be an important consideration. Such advantages as there might be in respect to wear would not be of any account, as the plates are not actually printed from ; they are only used for pulling proofs and transfers. The printing of editions direct from the plates is very rarely done nowadays ; it would be very costly, and there would be no object in it, since the lithographic method is so good and serves every purpose. Occasionally, an *edition de luxe* of the work of some famous composer may be printed direct, but in that case the number would be necessarily limited and the price charged proportional to the cost of printing.

Pewter plates have accordingly been universally

adopted for music engraving, and it does not seem likely that they will be displaced. Though commonly called " tin " plates more often than " pewter," they usually consist of an alloy of lead, tin, and antimony. The proportions given by one authority are : Lead, 8 parts ; tin, 1·5 parts ; antimony, 2 parts. In practice, however, the proportion of tin and antimony is varied according to the kind of music the plates are to be used for. Thus the engraver can choose a cheaper plate for work which may never run into a large edition nor have to be reprinted.

The following will show the variations which can be made in the formula for the alloy—

(a) Tin, 5 to 7·5 ; antimony, 2·5 to 5.
(b) Lead, 16 ; antimony, 1.
(c) Lead, 4 ; antimony, 2 ; zinc, 1.
(d) Lead, 7·5 ; antimony, 2·5 ; copper, 0·5.

We very much doubt whether copper or zinc is actually added to the alloy, but it might be there as an impurity, and the figures we have given may be the result of analysis.

We understand it is usual now to use a plate containing 35 to 40 per cent tin, the tendency being towards the former proportion on the ground of cheapness. At the present time, when tin is very dear, the proportion of this metal is probably still lower. Many foreign plates have been found to contain only about 10 per cent of tin, but such a low percentage is readily recognized, as the plates are slow in working owing to the difficulty of obtaining a sharp finish to the work.

83

Henri Robert, of Paris, gives the constituents of his plates as follows—

No. 1 Quality = 60 per cent tin
,,   2   ,,   = 46   ,,
,,   3   ,,   = 35   ,,
,,   4   ,,   = 20   ,,

He recommends a plate containing 35 per cent of tin for ordinary work, such as orchestral music, songs, and band parts ; whilst for more careful work, such as part songs and classical music, one with 46 per cent is better.

Sometimes plates prove crystalline owing to bad mixture of the alloy, and are difficult to punch, except when flowed with a film of oil, which seems to help matters.

In the old days when printing was done direct from the plates, they were harder ; and, even now, if direct printing is specified, harder plates are chosen. When it is known that the plates will be only used once, a soft alloy is often used.

Some of the old plates which have been analysed were found to have as much as 95 per cent of tin in them, so that it was quite justifiable to call them " tin " plates.

During the late European war, the Germans are reported to have melted down a large number of old stock music plates, no doubt on account of the large proportion of tin which they contained. English music publishers also disposed of a large number of plates during the war, tempted, no doubt, by the high price of metal at the time.

In a German publication it was stated that the firm

of C. G. Röder, the great music printers of Leipzig, employed about 200 engravers, and produced annually about 85,000 plates.

Another fact evidencing the extent to which music plates are used is that at a sale in London, in 1884, of the stock of a firm named Hutchings & Romer, 100,000 music plates were disposed of.

The best plates, it is stated, were supplied (before the war) by Bridault, of Paris ; but Cowles is an old-established London maker of music plates, who is still doing an extensive trade. This firm have a special alloy known as " Duffin's metal," which is much favoured.

The French plates are said to have been well finished and made with a fine quality of alloy. An American firm is also supplying very good music plates under the name of " Stanaloyd." Their plates are somewhat dearer than the English plates, but the quality of the metal and the excellent finish of the surface justifies it.

The pre-war cost of a plate 12 × 9 ins. of average quality was about 2s. 9d. In 1921 it was about the same, but the quality was inferior. The American plate of the same size costs 3s. 9d., according to a 1921 list, but a cheaper one has since been introduced.

The thickness of the plates is about ·05 in., and one side is polished.

There is a record of a patent taken out in 1861 for making pewter plates for music engraving by J. J. Watts and S. Harton. Watts was an electrotyper in Paternoster Square, and the author remembers his efforts to make plates by casting in the same way as

85

in making stereos. He states in his specification that he used an alloy of 7 parts tin, 7 parts lead, and 1 part antimony, the metal being poured in its molten state into a casting box fitted with a polished steel plate, so as to give a smooth surface to the cast. The back was no doubt planed in the usual way with a stereotyper's plate-shaving machine.

The plates as now supplied to the trade are ready for engraving upon, but if they show any scratches or irregularities on the surface through having become damaged, it is necessary to remove such imperfections by burnishing and, in extreme cases, also by scraping. This scraping is done by the "Busk," which is described in the next chapter. The burnishing is done by rubbing down any inequalities by means of the steel burnisher. Hollow places, pits, or deep scratches have to be beaten up, or punched up from the back. Sometimes the plate is given a final polish with fine emery paper, particularly when the plate shows scratches through the edge of the "busk" having been rough.

The plate sizes are usually smaller than the size of paper the music is to be printed on, as, of course, it is only necessary to cover the actual printed area.

The following are the usual stock sizes of plates—

9 × 6 inches	11½ × 8½ inches
9½ × 6½ ,,	12 × 9 ,,
10 × 7 ,,	13 × 9 ,,
10 × 7½ ,,	13 × 9½ ,,
10½ × 7½ ,,	13½ × 9½ ,,
11 × 8 ,,	

The two latter sizes are rarely used.

86

A 10 × 7 in. plate weighs about 1 lb. and, all sizes being the same thicknesses, their weights are proportional to the areas.

The 12 × 9 in. plate is used for songs and pianoforte pieces where bold printing is required, and the $11\frac{1}{2}$ × $8\frac{1}{2}$ in. for folio music.

The French sizes of plates are as follows—

Opera, 20 × 27 cm. ($7\frac{7}{8}$ × $10\frac{5}{8}$ ins.).
Symphony, 22 × 28 cm. ($8\frac{5}{8}$ × 11 ins.).
Grand Symphony, $22\frac{1}{2}$ × 30 cm. ($8\frac{7}{8}$ × $11\frac{3}{4}$ ins.).
Parts, $24\frac{1}{2}$ × 32 cm. ($9\frac{5}{8}$ × $12\frac{5}{8}$ ins.).
Conservatoire, $25\frac{1}{2}$ × 34 cm. (10 × $13\frac{3}{4}$ ins.).

CHAPTER VII

THE ENGRAVER'S TOOLS

IT is necessary for each workman to be provided with a set of tools for his individual use, apart from the punches, anvil, ruling board, scraping board, shoot plane and block, proof press, etc., which are provided by the employer.

The following constitutes the usual outfit—

Steel T-square.
Steel straight edge.
Scorers for the different sizes of staves.
Hook, or single tooth scorer, for single bar lines.
Two-line scorer for double bar lines.
Double scorer for the thick and thin lines for the initial brace of " full score " and choruses.
Marking pin, or drawing point.
Spring steel dividers.
Small brass compass.
Large brass compass.
Correcting callipers.
Levelling hammer.
Correcting hammer.
Striking hammer.
Scraper, known as the " busk."
Triangular steel scraper.
Steel burnisher.
Tint graver for the stems.
Lozenge graver for the slurs.
Elliptical graver for cutting swells.
Flat gravers of various sizes for the quaver ties.
Flat but narrow gravers for ledger lines.

We give illustrations and descriptions of these tools, and their use is fully described in the succeeding instructions.

The T-square (Fig. 38) is made of steel with a thin blade about 13 in. long by about $1\frac{1}{8}$ in. wide. The blade must be sufficiently flexible to enable it to be

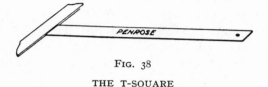

FIG. 38

THE T-SQUARE

pressed flat on the plate. The head should also be thin, so that it will not raise the blade above the surface of the plate. The blade is fixed centrally in the thickness of the head. There is thus a ledge on

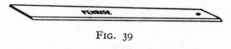

FIG. 39

THE STEEL STRAIGHT EDGE

both sides to lay up against the edge of the plate, and the square can thus be turned over so that both edges of the blade can be used and receive equal wear.

Some engravers do not use the steel straight edge (Fig. 39) but others use it in preference to the T-square when scoring the staves on the plate. It is about $\frac{1}{8}$ in. thickness, 12 ins. long, and one edge is bevelled. It need not be divided.

The scorer is one of the ·engraver's most important tools, and a great deal of the success of the work depends

89

on its quality. Whilst English engravers call it the "score" or "scorer," which is better to distinguish it from the score, as the stave is often called, the French call it the *tire-ligne* (literally "draw-line") and the Germans name it the *rasterale*.

As will be seen from Fig. 40, it is a kind of rake with five teeth, the points of which correspond to the distance between the stave lines. Naturally a different size of tool must be used for the nine different sizes of staves commonly used in music printing. The height of the staves varies from about

FIG. 40

THE SCORER

$\frac{1}{8}$ in. to about $\frac{3}{8}$ in., and the space between the teeth is one-fourth of the height of the stave, there being four spaces and five lines.

The staves for various sizes of music are numbered (Fig. 41.) These numbers are universal, so that if an English engraver sends an order to a foreign supplier of music tools for a scorer of a certain number, he will be sure to get the standard article. The numbers on the scorers do not, however, correspond to those of the music punches.

A very neat and useful scorer has been made with a universal holder and separate hook pieces for the different sizes of staves. (Fig. 42.)

The hook pieces have a square stem, which goes into a corresponding hole, and is clamped by means of a thumbscrew. This is said to be quite a practical

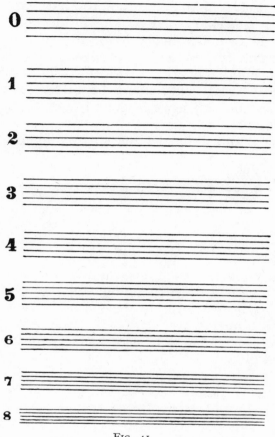

FIG. 41

SIZES OF MUSIC STAVES

tool and is very portable if the engraver has to do work away from the shop.

The scorer is a difficult tool to sharpen properly. The teeth are sharpened on the inside of the hook, which is held in the fingers over the edge of the oilstone, which is laid near the edge of the bench so that the handle of the tool can hang downwards. (Fig. 43.) Great care has to be taken to keep the face of the tool flat against the oilstone, so that there is no rounding off.

To meet this difficulty of sharpening the scorer,

FIG. 42

UNIVERSAL SCORER

ingenious devices have been made for maintaining the tool at the proper angle against the oilstone, but such appliances are rarely seen in use. A good form which is admitted by engravers to be very practical is shown in Fig. 44. The scorer is fixed in the clamp, which is placed over the oilstone so that the face to be sharpened rests on the stone. The rod on which the clamp is mounted is then pushed backwards and forwards, keeping the face of the tool firmly on the stone.

The hook (Fig. 45) is sometimes called the " single-line scorer," and is practically the same shape as the five-line tool, except that the hook is brought to a single point. It is used for cutting the single bar lines.

Some engravers of the old English school draw their stave lines with the single-toothed tool, using a ruling board, or setting out the space between the lines with the compass by pricking dots on the marginal lines, and using the T-square for guiding

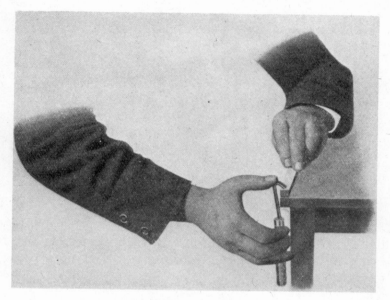

FIG. 43

METHOD OF SHARPENING THE SCORER

the tool. They say that they dislike the five-point tool because it requires more force for ruling the five lines at one time, and that it is often necessary to re-engrave some lines that are badly ruled.

French engravers use a tool similar to the " hook,"

93

which they call the " re-passing " tool, for clearing
or re-opening the lines.

A " two-line scorer " is sometimes employed to cut
two lines of equal thickness as required for double bar

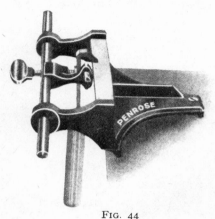

FIG. 44

SHARPENING DEVICE

lines.   These lines are often cut with the hook, after
being indicated with the marking pin, two cuts being
necessary.

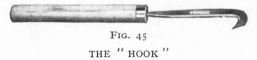

FIG. 45

THE " HOOK "

The double scorer (Fig. 46) cuts a thick and thin
line for the full score initial brace.

The marking pin (Fig. 47) is sometimes called the
drawing point.   It is made of steel rod about $\frac{1}{4}$ in.
thickness, tapering at each end to a fine but

94

well-rounded point, somewhat like a lead pencil. The pointed end must be very smooth, so that it does not scratch the plate, but only makes a mark such as a lead pencil would make on paper. The thick central part of the tool is twisted to enable the fingers to get a good grip on it. We have seen some engravers

FIG 46

THE DOUBLE SCORER

using a single-pointed tool with wooden handle, but the solid steel tool described above is more generally used. French engravers use a tool with one end pointed and the other end shaped as a burnisher,

FIG. 47

THE MARKING PIN

presumably to erase with the burnisher any sign marked wrongly.

The marking pin is used for showing the position of the notes and indicating the kind of notes or signs to be punched. The method of marking is described in the next chapter. The tool is also used for indicating the marginal lines which form the limits of the engraving and for showing the position of the bars to be engraved.

The spring steel dividers (Fig. 48) are used for spacing the ledger lines, and also by some engravers for marking out the position of the staves on the marginal lines so as to obtain the correct spacing between the staves when the ruling is done by a single-toothed score hook. The screw adjustment to the legs of the divider ensures that there is no shifting of the points, as there might be with the brass compass.

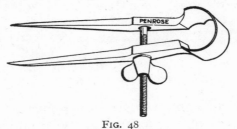

FIG. 48

SPRING STEEL DIVIDERS

For setting out the spaces between the notes and bars, a small brass compass of the ordinary pattern adopted by draughtsmen is used. It is about 4 in.

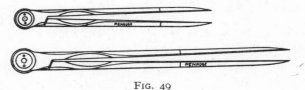

FIG. 49

BRASS COMPASS

in length over all, and the joint should be stiff so that there is no risk of slipping. The points are sharp, as it is necessary they should make an indentation in the plate. A longer brass compass is also useful for setting out the staves. (Fig. 49.)

Two forms of callipers are shown. Fig. 51 is the

older pattern, and is still used ; but the more modern German pattern (Fig. 50) is held by many engravers to be preferable, as there is not the liability to get the points out of alignment with each other.

The callipers are used, as will be described fully

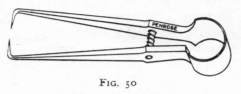

FIG. 50

CORRECTING CALLIPERS

in the next chapter, for making a mark on the back of the plate exactly opposite to the note or sign which has to be corrected, and thus shows the part which

FIG 51

has to be hammered or punched up on the back of the plate.

The levelling hammer (Fig. 52) is used when knocking up the plate on the anvil for levelling or flattening.

The correcting hammer is the same shape as the levelling hammer, but is lighter.

The engraver uses this hammer to tap down any parts which have become bulged in the punching, using the hammer on the face of the plate whilst the latter is resting on the stone. The face of the hammer is slightly convex, so that there is not any risk of making hammer marks by an experienced engraver. The plate is often turned over during the punching,

97

so as to tap up any parts from the back and to keep the surface level. Occasionally the small rounded end of the hammer is used to localize the tapping up. Engravers have each their own special preference as to the shape of the shaft of the hammer, some

FIG. 52

THE LEVELLING HAMMER

preferring a straight oval shape like an ordinary carpenter's hammer, whilst others like the turned shape shown in the illustration.

Fig. 53 shows the usual form of the striking hammer or mallet (as the French term it) for striking the

FIG. 53

THE STRIKING HAMMER

punches, but some workers of the old English school prefer to employ the head of an ordinary carpenter's hammer of suitable weight and with a short handle. The wedge-shaped end of the head is kept rounded and highly burnished, so that it can be used for rubbing down any part of the plate which needs such treatment.

It is held by some engravers that it is better to have two striking hammers, one a little heavier than the other, for striking the large characters, rather than to give the heavier blow which would be needed with the ordinary hammer.

A flexible piece of steel (Fig. 54), about 5 in. in length by 1¼ in. width (known as the " busk ") is used

FIG. 54

THE " BUSK " SCRAPER

for scraping the plate to bring up a good surface. It is used somewhat in the same way as a cabinet-maker's scraper on wood, except that its flexibility allows it to be curved, and this allows a localized scraping to be done.

The triangular scraper (Fig. 55) is one of the engraver's most important tools, and particular pains

FIG. 55

THE TRIANGULAR SCRAPER

are taken in selecting it and keeping a proper edge on it. Formerly, the engraver made the tool himself from an old triangular saw file, and no doubt many still do so, but it is hardly worth while when a really good article can be obtained cheaply. It is said that the German makers of music engravers' tools, before the war, used worn-out English files for making the scrapers, because of the excellent quality of the

99

steel ; but our files are not so good as they used to be, so that probably there is not the same inducement. It is a matter of surprise how the Germans could sell the scrapers so cheaply, as the price charged does not seem enough to pay for the labour of grinding them ; but, of course, if they were able to get discarded files very cheaply, that is a possible explanation.

If the scraper is made from an old file, the first step is to grind off the teeth and hollow grind the surfaces until the tool has somewhat the appearance of an old-style bayonet. The sides look like a hollow-

FIG. 56

THE BURNISHER

ground razor, and the edges must be made very keen. The curve of the hollow sides in the best scrapers we have seen has a radius of about 4 in., but an old engraver who grinds his own scrapers says he makes the hollow fit a five-shilling piece. The blade should be 6½ to 7 in. length over all, and it is mounted on a suitable wooden handle, some preferring a straight cylindrical handle, others a curved handle.

The tool is practically identical with the bayonet scraper used by copperplate engravers, though larger and heavier, and one of these would probably answer the purpose if the proper article is not available.

The burnisher is equally as important a tool as the scraper. It is used for polishing the surface of the plate and for closing up any parts which have been punched or engraved too deeply. It is also used in

100

locally finishing the surface before and after corrections. The blade is about 4 in. long and is very highly polished. It must be carefully preserved in this state.

The tint graver (Fig. 57) is similar to that used by wood and copper-plate engravers, and the blade is

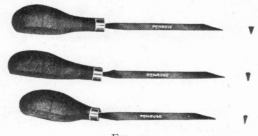

FIG. 57

TINT GRAVERS

in the form of a very acute V. A rather longer face is ground on it than would be used by the copper-plate engraver, making the angle with the back more acute, so that it readily enters without any tendency

FIG. 58

THE LOZENGE GRAVER

to drag the metal out. The back is slightly curved. The tool is used for cutting fine lines, such as the stems of the notes.

The lozenge graver (Fig. 58) has a more obtuse V-shape in the blade than the tint graver. It is, in fact, in the form of a complete lozenge in section, the lower of the two acute angles being used for the cutting. Naturally, from its shape, it cuts a broader line than the tint graver, and the more deeply it is forced into the metal, the more broadly it cuts. It is used for engraving the slurs, for which the tool must enter lightly, penetrate more deeply for the middle

FIG. 59

THE ELLIPTICAL GRAVER

part of the curve, and run out lightly. The engraver acquires the facility of doing this by practice.

The blade of Fig. 59 is of elliptical form, making a section which would be a V with bowed sides. A good engraver can vary the thickness of the line with

FIG. 60

THE FLAT GRAVER

this tool, which works very smoothly. It is principally used for cutting the " swells."

Flat gravers have parallel sides, cutting like a chisel, so that the line is of the same thickness as the tool, and the bottom of the cut is flat. These tools are used for cutting the ties of the connected quavers. Several sizes are required to suit the different sizes of notes, the ties being thickened in proportion to the size. Flat but narrow gravers are also used for cutting the ledger lines.

102

There is another form of graver often used, known as the "Trotter." A wood engraver would call it a knife graver. It has a very thin blade ground to a knife-like edge, and the end of the blade is ground off at a right angle to the back. It is used by some engravers to precede the scorer when the lines are ruled again after planishing, the object being to prevent the scorer running out of the lines.

A variety of other sizes and shapes of gravers is obtainable, but the above forms a sufficient assortment for the beginner and probably as many as the "old hand" cares to use.

There is a difference of opinion as to the best form of handle for the gravers. Some we have seen from a French maker have a long pear-shaped handle, with or without the under side flattened. The shape more generally approved is the mushroom pattern (as Fig. 60), with the underside cut away to form a flat, so as to clear the plate and enable the engraver to keep the blade more nearly level to the surface. Those who use this pattern also think it best because the tip of the little finger can be held in the hollow under the ball of the handle.

The shop tools, such as the anvil, scraping board, etc., will be described in a later chapter dealing with the use of them.

CHAPTER VIII

THE PUNCHES

THE steel punches on which are cut the musical notes, signs, and letters, constitute the principal part of the music engraver's outfit. A set of punches consists usually of from fifty to fifty-five pieces. The steel shank on which the character is cut is generally from $2\frac{1}{2}$ to 3 in. in length and about $\frac{1}{4}$ in. to $\frac{5}{16}$ in. in square section. Large characters necessitate greater dimensions to give strength to withstand the blow and also to afford a larger face. The punches for the brackets, clefs, slurs, etc., are enlarged at the end as requisite. For the smaller notes and signs, the punches are tapered down to the end, so that the position of the point on the plate can be readily seen.

A nick on one side of the punch indicates the direction in which the punch should be held to enable the character to be punched the right way up. The nick indicates the bottom of the sign or letter, and is always next the thumb when the punch is held correctly. (Fig. 61.) The temper of the punches is indicated by a yellow or blue shade from stem to point. The cutting is somewhat shallow, and the bottom of the cut is flat.

Fig. 62 shows the appearance of a set of punches. They are usually held in perforated wooden blocks

104

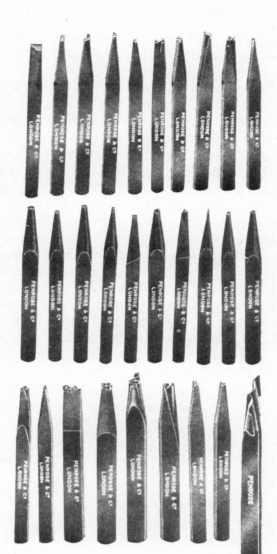

FIG. 61

PUNCH,
SHOWING
NICK ON
SIDE

FIG. 62
THE PUNCHES

105

or boxes, with their points uppermost and a sufficient distance apart so that the engraver can readily pick them out. (Fig. 63.)

There are twelve sizes of punches catalogued by the makers, covering all sizes of music, but not more than eight sizes are generally used, and, as a rule, a range of six or seven sizes are found sufficient. Fig. 64 illustrates the various sizes comparatively.

It should be noted that the numbers of the punches do not correspond to the numbers of the scores. To avoid confusion the Germans not only give a number to each size of punches, but also a name, as shown in abbreviated form at the side of the examples. (Page 108.)

"Stempel Zeug" is stamping tool, "Maho" and "Peter" probably refers to certain well-known music albums or instruction books, "Gewöhnlich" is ordinary, "Grosse Mittel" and "Kleine Mittel" means large medium and small medium. "Pearl" corresponds to a very small size of printer's type.

The following list describes the purpose for which the various score sizes are used—

Nos. 1 and 2. For tutors and orchestral music.
No. 3. Songs and pianoforte (sheet music).
 ,, 4. Songs and pianoforte (albums).
 ,, 5. Band parts and operatic music.
 ,, 6. Part songs.
 ,, 7. Pocket editions, and for violin " cue " lines in piano and violin pieces.
 ,, 8. Thematic advertisements and incidental purposes.

No. 1 is known in the trade as the " Giant " size, and is seldom used. Nos. 3, 4, 6, and 7 are usually reckoned sufficient for the engraving of most of the usual styles of music. The very small sizes are rarely used. If a very small size is required, as for the miniature reproductions of music pages in publishers' announcements on the back of pieces, it is easy to punch a larger size, take a proof, and reproduce it as a zinco block.

Whilst the employer usually provides the punches, the engraver generally prefers to have a set of slur punches of his own, as they are not expensive, rather than have to be constantly getting them from other engravers who may be using them. There are about

FIG. 63

BLOCK FOR HOLDING PUNCHES

eleven sizes. A set of braces for the different sizes of staves is also required, these being usually provided by the employer.

Besides the punches for the notes and signs, various sets of punches for lettering are also required. There being such a variety of styles of type, it is impossible to say what types ought to be employed. Usually it is a matter of taste, decided by the publisher who often wants a distinctive style for his publications. For the words of songs, there are certain standards that are common to all countries, and the punches for these are catalogued either by number to indicate size, and by such typographical descriptions as Roman, italic, etc., to designate style. The numbers

FIG. 64

St. Z. 1 = Stempel Zeug No. 1
Maho Z 2 = Maho Zeug No. 2
Gew. Z 3 = Gewöhnlich Zeug No. 3
Pet. Z 4 = Peter Zeug No. 4
Gr. M. Z 5 = Grosse Mittel Zeug No. 5
Kl. M. Z 6 = Kleine Mittel Zeug No. 6
Cad. Z 7 = Cadenza Zeug No. 7
Perl. Z 8 = Pearl Zeug No. 8

108

bear no relation to typographic point sizes. For instance, No. 4 in type for music engraving refers to a letter about ⅛ in. in height, whilst a 4-point letter in typography would be less than half this size. The lettering punches usually follow typographic styles, and very seldom is a new " face " created by the punch cutters unless demanded.

It may be thought strange that titles are not set up in type, or drawn by a lithographic artist and transferred with the music ; but it seems to be preferred to have them either punched or engraved, probably in order that the appearance will harmonize with that of the music print. Moreover, it is cheaper and saves time.

The writer is informed that before the war there were no English makers of music punches, but there are now two punch-cutters : Sale, in Birmingham ; and Marchant, in London. The trade has been almost entirely held hitherto by the German makers located chiefly in Leipzig, the great centre of music printing. They have supplied beautifully finished tools in great variety and very cheaply. If any special punches were required, these firms were always ready to make them at a slight advance on the price of the existing stock ones. It is said that as the native steel was not good enough, the German toolmaker was shrewd enough to get the right metal from Sheffield. The writer is informed that the German tools have always been considered good in hardness, in finish, and in clean deeply-cut quality. They were, moreover, remarkably cheap at pre-war prices, and British manufacturers, who were asked if they could imitate them, could not see how the tools could be produced at the price. The reason was that the German makers had a wide sale for their tools, not only at home, but in other countries, and thus could produce them in quantity with the aid of specially constructed machinery.

Some French makers have supplied excellent tools, which are well tempered—even better in this respect than some of the German tools—but there was a prejudice against them here, because German engravers had spread the reputation of the tools of their own country and, being of indisputably fine quality, the English workman had been led to believe there was nothing to equal them.

The tools of Henri Robert are undoubtedly good ; and L. Gordon is another French maker, whose punches are acceptable, though the design of the notes and signs on the French punches is not so much liked as the German style.

We have heard it stated that the reason the German tools are so smoothly finished is that they were not tempered so hard as the French ones. On the other hand, engravers who have used the German tools say they have no fault to find with the hardness, and that the tools will last a lifetime with ordinary care.

It was possible before the war to send punches back to the German makers to be re-cut or re-faced, and this was done at half the cost of new tools. In some cases it was possible for the engraver to level the face of a punch by rubbing it carefully on an oilstone, taking care to hold the stem vertically.

A good set of letter punches costs from £5 to £7,

according to size and the intricacy of the characters. This price would include a set of punctuation marks.

The music punches are sold in sets of fifty-two or fifty-five, and the No. 8 size is dearer than Nos. 1 to 7. A French maker quotes, at the time of writing, £7 for a set of fifty-five music punches.

A well-known German maker of repute is Otto Rühl, who has been making music punches for the last twenty years. He has quoted, early in 1922, Marks 3,120 for a set of fifty-two punches in Nos. 1 to 7 sizes, or Marks 3,500 for No. 8.

Alphabets and figures are usually priced by the punch. The above German maker quotes 75 to 90 marks each, and a French maker the equivalent of from 2s. 6d. to 5s. 6d. each. Figures are charged at the same price as letters, and punctuation marks at half price. Title letters vary from 60 to 75 marks each, say 2s. 3d. to 2s. 9d. Of course, prices quoted in marks may be subject to wide fluctuations in price, according to the rate of exchange, and the expenses of transport have to be added. Moreover, the German punch cutters have been repeatedly advancing their prices owing to increased wages and rising cost of materials, so that there is no advantage in buying from Germany. A Munich punch cutter was, early in 1922, quoting £7 in English money for a set of music punches.

Penrose's, London, who are now stocking punches, give in their latest catalogue, 2s. 9d. each as average price for note punches, a set of fifty-two costing about £7 ; and 2s. to 3s. for letter and figure punches. Complete sets are about £7 to £7 10s.

Slur punches are sold singly at 2s. 6d. each, or in sets at about £1. Brackets, also, are supplied in sets at 25s. per set, or singly at from 3s. to 3s. 6d. each.

Word punches are charged at about 1s. 6d. per letter.

CHAPTER IX

PRELIMINARIES TO ENGRAVING

THE engraver having received the manuscript copy of the music to be engraved, has to mark it off, sometimes called " casting off." The manuscript is not always neatly written and spaced out so as to be easy for the engraver to copy it. In fact, manuscript music is sometimes as crabbed and illegible as the handwriting of authors, and is just as variable in its characteristics. The greater the genius of the composer, the more likely that his composition is hastily scribbled and full of corrections. It is for the engraver to impart to it the necessary neatness of arrangement to suit it for printing.

The first step is to decide upon the number of pages the piece will make, and thereby determine how many plates it will be necessary to engrave. If the number of pages is limited by the publisher, it may be necessary to close up the notes ; whilst, on the other hand, a short piece may have the notes spread out in order to fill the required number of pages.

The nature of the music to be engraved will indicate the number of notes to be contained in a line of the printed music. The bars necessary to give this number of notes are marked in pencil on the manuscript, according to whatever scheme is decided on. The total number of lines to be engraved is thus easily reckoned, and the number of plates required is readily determined by dividing the number of lines to be engraved by the number of lines that will go on a plate.

The first plate contains two or three lines less than the subsequent ones, because it is necessary to reserve a space for the title, the names of the author and composer, and perhaps for a dedication.

A very important point in the marking-off is to find a convenient place to turn over at the foot of an odd numbered page. Such a suitable place is, for instance, when there is a rest, allowing time to turn over without being obliged to break the phrase. It is sometimes necessary to close up a little the preceding lines or, on the other hand, to extend them in order to provide a turnover. It is usual, also, to arrange for the last line of a piece to be filled up, although an even distribution of the matter is preferable.

Naturally, the size of page determines the marking-off, and here it may be remarked that the absence of any standards in the sizes of English music is a serious drawback which the trade might very well join in remedying.

To the general public, it may seem that what is known as " sheet music " for songs and pianoforte is uniform in size, but anyone who attempts to bind up a number of pieces of sheet music will find there is a considerable discrepancy in size between the pieces issued by different publishers. Actually, it may be said there are as many sizes as there are publishers, for each firm appears to have its own standards of size. Equally variable are the measurements of the printed matter on the pages. This will be evident from the following measurements of piano size music selected at random from half a dozen different publishers—

Trimmed size of paper. Inches.	Measurement of printed matter. Inches.
$14\frac{1}{2} \times 10\frac{1}{4}$	$12\frac{3}{4} \times 8\frac{5}{8}$
$14\frac{1}{8} \times 10\frac{1}{8}$	$12\frac{3}{4} \times 8\frac{1}{2}$
14×10	$12\frac{7}{8} \times 8\frac{5}{8}$
$14 \times 10\frac{1}{8}$	$10\frac{5}{8} \times 7\frac{5}{8}$
$13\frac{3}{8} \times 10\frac{5}{8}$	$10\frac{1}{2} \times 7\frac{1}{2}$
$13\frac{1}{4} \times 10\frac{1}{8}$	$11\frac{1}{4} \times 8$

As we have said, each house seems to have its own standards of size, and this appears to be actually so according to inquiries we have made. Augener's edition is $12\frac{1}{4} \times 9\frac{1}{4}$ in., which, as will be seen, is smaller than the average English piano size.

Messrs. Lowe & Brydone, who print a large amount of pianoforte music and songs, state that their full music size is trimmed to 14×10 in. Their music octavo is half the size, 10×7 in. These two sizes require a special size of paper, $28\frac{1}{2} \times 20\frac{1}{2}$ in., called " Double Music," being different from any of the regular printers' sizes. Some other kinds of music are, however, done on standard sizes of printing papers ; for instance, albums are printed by this firm on royal quarto and also at times on demy quarto.

Messrs. Curwen & Son use a sheet known as " double music size," measuring $28\frac{1}{2} \times 20\frac{3}{4}$ in., from which they get the sheet music for piano or song ($14\frac{1}{4} \times 10\frac{3}{8}$ in.), which, when trimmed down, would be the usual fraction over 14×10 in. Their octavo from the same sheet is $10\frac{3}{8} \times 7\frac{1}{8}$ in. The firm have a special size known as " music royal " ($37\frac{1}{2} \times 25$ in.), nearly approaching printers' double royal, which is 40 × 25 in. This is also cut or folded to quarto ($12\frac{1}{2}$ × $9\frac{3}{8}$ in.).

Messrs. Novello & Co. specialize in certain sizes, in particular, their octavo editions, which are in super-royal octavo. Super-royal is $27\frac{1}{2}$ × $20\frac{1}{2}$ in., so that the sheet, when folded into eight pages, is $9\frac{1}{2}$ × $6\frac{11}{16}$ in. This size is used for oratorios.

CHAPTER X

RULING THE STAVES

THE first step towards the engraving is the ruling of marginal lines on the plate to determine the limits of the engraving.

A line is scratched round the four sides of the plate by means of the steel T-square and drawing point, or by the dividers, drawing one leg against the side of the T-square. The square should be first applied to the edges of the plate to see if the sides are correctly at right angles to each other. If they are not, the fault should be remedied by trimming the edges with a plane and shoot-block. (Fig. 65.) By using a ruling board, this is unnecessary, as the plate can be ruled independently of the squareness or otherwise of the edges.

Assuming the plate is found to be square, the T-square can be applied to the side and a line ruled about $\frac{1}{4}$ in. from the edge, which will form the left-hand side of the plate. The line on the right-hand side should allow a little more margin if a bracket is to be inserted.

It must be noted that the engraving has to be made reversed, reading from right to left, to allow for transferring, which reverses the image again. The space at the top of the plate should be a little more than at the bottom.

The next step is to indicate the points where the staves commence and finish. The staves are not always at the same distance apart, as space has to be allowed for the ledger lines. By examining the manuscript, it will be seen which staves should have their distance apart varied.

By means of the dividers, the number and position

FIG. 65

THE SHOOT BLOCK

of the staves is set out on the right-hand marginal line, the points of the dividers being lightly pressed into the plate within the scratched line. The spacing between the lines of the stave is indicated by means of the scorer. The first tooth of the tool is placed on the dot made by the compass point, and the five teeth are then pressed firmly into the traced marginal line. The operation is repeated for the other staves

118

and then the points thus laid down are repeated on the left-hand line exactly opposite. The points thus impressed serve to stop the tool when it comes to the end of the stave when ruling.

If no ruling board is available, the scorer is guided

FIG. 66

METHOD OF USING THE SCORER

by the T-square or straight edge, but it is essential in that case that the sides of the plates are square to each other. The plate is placed with the right-hand margin at the top, furthest away from the engraver. The T-square is laid with its head against the same side of the plate, so that the scorer is drawn vertically towards the engraver. The square is placed against the points indicating the fifth or top line of the first stave. The left hand firmly presses on the square so that it will not shift, and the scorer is grasped with the right hand, the index finger pressing against the top of the tool. (Fig. 66 shows the correct position of the hands.) The left-hand tooth of the tool is dropped into the point indicating the first line. The other four teeth are then dropped into the

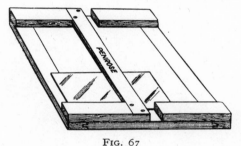

FIG. 67

RULING BOARD

remaining points and, when it is felt that all the teeth are pressing equally on the plate, the tool is drawn lightly forward, taking care to maintain an equal pressure on it. The five dents impressed on the opposite marginal line serve to indicate when to stop the tool. The tool is drawn through the five lines thus made four or five times, in order to obtain sufficiently deep cuts, and to ensure the lines being of equal strength.

If no five-point score tool is available, or if it is preferred to rule the lines singly, the single line

120

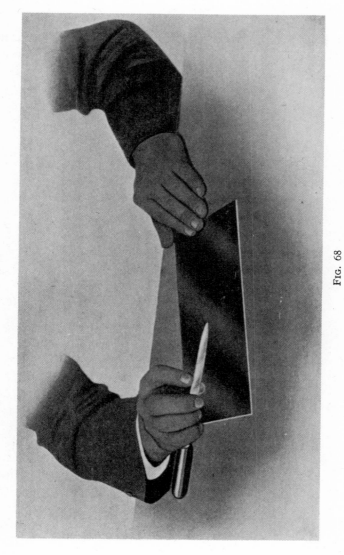

FIG. 68

METHOD OF USING THE TRIANGULAR SCRAPER

tool is used against the T-square or on a ruling board.

The ruling board (Fig. 67) is a convenience in ruling the staves, though it is not generally used. It consists of a board somewhat larger than the largest

FIG. 69

SCRAPING WITH THE " BUSK "

plate to be used, and across it is a steel rule screwed to strips at the side, these strips being slightly thicker than the plate, which can therefore be pushed under the rule. The plate is firmly held against one of the side strips, whilst the score tool is drawn over it, guided by the steel rule. This board can be used

122

either with the single-toothed tool or the five-pointed tool.

One advantage of using the ruling board is that the engraver can work independently of any want of squareness of the sides of the plate, which would otherwise have to be remedied by a shoot-block and squaring plane, found in some shops.

It should be noted that at the head of a piece, or where the *motif* changes, a part of the stave has an indent, leaving a place for such words as " Piano," " Song," " Introduction." These words should be placed opposite the middle of the bracket or stave lines.

On passing the finger over the lines that have been ruled, a burr will be felt, and it is necessary to remove this with the triangular scraper, which should be held as shown in Fig. 68.

The scraping should be lightly done, in a direction askew to the lines, without cutting deeply into the surface of the plate. A final scraping is given with the " busk " before commencing to mark the plate. Fig. 69 shows how the " busk " is held.

CHAPTER XI

MARKING THE PLATE

WE now come to a very important stage in the engraving of the music plate, known as the marking, or drawing, or writing as it is sometimes called.

The purpose of this operation is to show the position and character of the notes to be punched. The kind of note or sign is shown by certain well understood marks, forming a sort of shorthand for the music engraver. Fig. 70 shows the form of the marks generally used.

We also give a reproduction (Figs. 71 and 72) showing the appearance of a plate after it has been marked out. The marks are lightly drawn on the plate by means of the marking pin, giving a pencil effect. It is not necessary to give any great exactness of form or size of the notes, but simply a sufficient indication to enable each note to be recognized so as to avoid any error in punching.

The notes which are to be on the lines are designated by a circle, no matter whether they are crotchets, minims, or semibreves ; and those which are in the spaces are indicated by a sign which is similar to the written letter N. To distinguish the value of each note, a cross is made through the circle for the semibreve and a single line through for the

124

minims, the circle being left without any mark for the crotchets. The quavers have their hooks or ties shown.

Various workers have their own way of indicating the notes, but the above is typical of the general system adopted. This way of drawing the notes in marking out is not merely a conventional thing, but a necessity in order that any workman can punch a plate drawn by another man.

The marking is accompanied by spacing out the notes, and it should be remarked that this is a

FIG. 70

ENGRAVERS' MARKS

work which requires considerable experience. A well-engraved piece of music ought to give the player at a glance a general idea of the movement. The space assigned to the notes should be proportional to their value. Thus the semibreve should have more space than the minim and the latter more than the crotchet. In the same degree, the spacing for the other notes should be regulated correctly. The quavers, which are played rapidly, ought to present to the eye a more closed-up appearance. With songs and choruses, allowance must be made for the length of the syllable in conjunction with the note value.

The marking is of primary importance in pianoforte music, scores, and choruses ; and in all high-class music particular attention should be given to this part of the work. In orchestral or military band

125

FIG. 71

APPEARANCE OF A MARKED OUT PLATE

FIG. 72

THE FINISHED PLATE

music such exactitude in the marking out can be dispensed with if sufficient symmetry is put into the spacing. Of course, it is necessary to avoid commencing wide and finishing close, or *vice versa.*

The work of marking is one which is generally taught last of all to the apprentice-engraver, but we describe it here so as to keep to the sequence of the work in the order of its execution. The beginner will have to learn punching and engraving before he learns marking.

This part of the work really requires some knowledge of music, as it is necessary, if errors are to be avoided, to know the rules as to the placing of clefs, notes, signs, etc., on their proper lines or in the proper spaces. It is not within the scope of this book to give these rules, which can be learnt from any elementary manual explaining the musical notation. A study of good examples of printed music is also helpful.

It is necessary to indicate on the plate absolutely all that is in the manuscript, so that nothing is forgotten in the punching and cutting, and the indications must be distinct. The engraver does not have the manuscript in front of him for guidance in striking and cutting : he merely follows the indications on the plate.

In proceeding with the marking of the plate, the experienced engraver, after a moment's consideration of the amount " laid out " for a line on the manuscript, selects a note which seems to predominate, usually a crotchet or a quaver ; and, guided by his experience only, decides to allow so much for the selected note. He then proceeds with the indication of the spacing on the plate. The actual amount of space is largely a matter of guesswork, a method of " trial and error." He may have to make two or three attempts before the line is accurately set out.

The indication of the spacing is done by what is termed " pointing." For this purpose, the small brass compass is used to make dots on the plate corresponding to the spaces required Taking the plate with the stave lines ruled and scraped, the engraver proceeds as follows : First, a guide line for the clef is ruled all the way down the plate by means of the T-square and marking pin, or by holding one leg of the compass against the side of the plate and setting the other leg to the required position. The distance from the ends of the stave lines is one space (i.e. the space between two of the stave lines). At this point a line is drawn the height of the stave to indicate the position for the clef, which should touch this line. Then from the clef another line is drawn at a distance equal to the height of the stave, and against this line is marked the first of the key signatures, if any. Should there be none, then the actual spacing for the music begins here. Suppose there are two sharps, then the first receives one space value, but the second a space equal to the height of the stave. The rule is that the music is separate from the last guide line of the above signs by the width of the scorer.

The pointing then follows. The engraver sets the legs of the compass to the amount he judges should be the space between the notes and, holding the compass

in his fingers as shown in the illustration (Fig. 73),
he rapidly twirls it from one point to the other, lifting
it from the plate only when allowing more or less
space until he reaches the end of the line. Each
time he presses the points on the plate he makes a
dot which indicates the spacing. If the first attempt

FIG. 73
POINTING WITH THE COMPASS

does not seem successful, the compass is re-set and the
pointing done again under the first line of dots. The
dotting is done in a space or upon one of the stave lines.

Finally, the guide lines are drawn through each
dot in the successful line of spacing, and against the
lines are marked the notes, etc.

The French method of pointing is different in that

130

instead of guesswork the distance between two lines in the stave or, in other words, between two teeth of the scorer, is taken as a unit, and the engraver mentally counts the number of space units he will allow between the notes, also allowing one or more spaces for the notes and signs. It is more easy for the beginner in music engraving to have a definite amount to give for the spacing, but the experienced engraver does not need such aid.

It must be clearly understood that whichever system is adopted, the chosen amount should represent a given musical value, increasing or diminishing according to the time. Thus an addition or subtraction of spacing must be made whenever a note is encountered of greater or lesser value than the one chosen as predominant. For example, if the spacing is set for a crotchet, one more space must be allowed when a minim is encountered. A dotted (augmented) minim requires two spaces more, a quaver one less, a semiquaver two less, and so on. There is always a small space left between each bar line and the first note of the bar, equal to rather more than one space.

The rests have the same importance as the notes of the same value, and are given the same spacing. The accidentals occupy one space.

For drawing the ledger lines, the spring dividers are opened to the full height of the stave, and the points of the legs are placed in the first and fifth lines, being pressed into the lines rather strongly. In drawing a first ledger line above the stave, one point of the dividers is placed in the second line of the

131

stave, this serving as a guide for drawing the ledger line parallel, using the other point for lightly scratching the line. If a ledger line is to be drawn below the stave, one point of the dividers is placed on the fourth line of the stave. The same is done for the other ledger lines, shifting the guiding point of the dividers up or down the stave. The lines are only lightly scratched by the compass points. The cutting of these lines will be described later.

Ruling the bars is done at the same time as the guide lines by means of the T-square placed with its head against the edge of the plate at the top, and the blade in line with the indentations made by the pointing. The vertical lines cutting through the points are then traced.

We have endeavoured to give the general principles governing the marking. These, however, can be varied according to the different cases which present themselves ; sometimes, for instance, by the necessity of closing up, in order to allow for a larger number of notes, or, on the other hand, the proportions may be reduced for a less number. At other times, the space being wide, it is necessary to treat it accordingly. These different cases are often brought about by the necessity of arriving at a convenient turnover. In any case, the eye is often the best judge for the placing of each value properly ; in fact, a good many engravers use no other guide.

LETTERING.

For the words of songs, or any other lettering that is to appear on the plates, it is necessary to carefully

132

mark out the position. With the marking pin or compass point and the T-square, a line is traced to serve as a base for the lettering. It is desirable that this should be a fine sharp line. If the lettering consists of words to the music, the exact place of each syllable must be indicated.

The spacing is done with due regard to both the musical value of the notes and the length of the syllable beneath. Therefore, when the engraver marks out a plate on which the words of a song are to be given under the stave, he has to consider not only the spacing suitable for the notes but also for the syllables which are written on the plate underneath in approximately the position the letters will be struck. Lines are sometimes ruled on the plate to guide the engraver in striking the letters in exact alignment, but an experienced engraver does not need this help.

Where there are verses apart from the music, the position reserved for them is set out. In cheap music the verses are placed underneath the music on the same page, but in better class music a separate page preceding the music is allotted to them.

Usually the verses are placed in two columns, and the first step is to draw a centre line to divide the page or part of the page on which the verses are to appear. Then the engraver finds the average length of the text line, and from that determines the space to allow in the margin. A vertical line is then drawn on the plate, or two lines if each alternate text line is indented. The laws of rhythm, of course, govern the indenting. Where there is a chorus, a third line must be ruled to indicate the position for starting the words, as the chorus has often longer or shorter lines than the verses. On these marginal lines, dots are made with the compass to indicate the space between the text lines, and lines are then ruled as a base for placing the punches.

TITLES.

The title lines demand much taste on the part of the engraver if an agreeable effect is to be produced. It is necessary that the position of the letters should be carefully set out. In the middle of the space reserved for the title, a perpendicular line is drawn on which the various heights of the type it is desired to use are indicated; then the base lines for the different rows of lettering are drawn. The number of letters in the principal lines are counted and half of them are placed on each side of the middle line, due allowance being made for an I being narrow, or a W or M being broad, when the central letter is selected. This central letter is then struck, the next being placed to the right or left of it.

The author's name is usually in letters half the height of the title line, but tastes vary in this respect In order to judge the effect of a title, it is often struck first on a trial plate; but this is a part of the punching operations, and is described in the next chapter.

It may be stated here that title lines are usually punched, not only because the work harmonizes better in " colour " with the rest of the plate, but also because it is quicker than engraving. There are, however, occasions when a title is engraved, possibly because some special style is wanted, for which no punches are available.

In the best music there is an outside title on the cover, an inside title on page 1, the verses being given on page 2 in case of a song, and the music commencing on page 3.

CHAPTER XII

THE PUNCHING

FOR the punching, or " striking " as it is often called, the plate is laid on a thick slab, usually a lithographic stone, measuring about 14×13 in. and from 2 to 3 in. in thickness. The surface must be very smooth and level without any indentations. This stone rests on a solid wooden bench of such height as will enable the workman to sit comfortably at his work. Naturally, the bench is somewhat low, as he must be able to look directly down on his plate, and the height of the stone has to be allowed for. The bench is preferably placed against a window. When music engraving is done by artificial light, the ordinary electric lamp pendant is brought down level with the head of the engraver and the light shaded from his eyes.

To perform the operation of punching properly, it is essential that the workman should be seated properly with the plate directly in front of him and central to the body, so that he has not to incline himself either to the right or the left. It is upon the correctness of his position that the regularity of the punching depends.

The punch is held in the left hand between the thumb and the first and second fingers, the nicked side being next the thumb. The side of the little

136

finger should rest freely on the plate to support the hand. Fig. 74 illustrates the position of the hand and punch. The head of the punch should first be slightly inclined towards the workman, with the

FIG. 74

METHOD OF STRIKING THE PUNCH

bottom edge of the sign caught against the guiding line on the plate.

In the case of notes in the spaces, this guiding line is the stave line below it ; but for notes to be struck on the lines, the engraver locates the position for the punch by means of a raised line on the face of the

137

punch. All note punches (at least all modern ones) have a centre guide line raised above the face and crossing the note centrally. Minims have a small tick raised in the centre of the widest part. The engraver has only to drop this raised line or tick into the score line to be sure that the note will be in the correct position.

Where punches are not provided with this raised part, a stroke can be scratched half-way in the space below the line to form a guide for placing the punch, but the experienced engraver usually relies on judgment alone.

Having placed the punch against the line, it is brought to a vertical position and, whilst held perpendicularly, a smart blow is given on the head of the punch with the striking mallet or hammer.

The depth of the impression should not be much more than $\frac{1}{64}$ in., and the force of the blow must be such as to secure this depth uniformly for all characters. It is also necessary to proportion the force of the blow in accordance with the size of the sign to be struck, for it is conceivable that more force is needed to punch a clef than to punch a note-head.

The musical signs offer very little difficulty in punching, but not so with the lettering, which requires most practice to obtain regularity of appearance, so as to equal the symmetry of type composition. In punching the text, the letters should be closed up as much as possible, but not so close as to cause the last letter struck to deform the preceding one.

PUNCHING TITLES.

The letter is first indicated by a very light blow, in order to see if it is well placed and straight, and so that it can be rectified if necessary. Then with a blow of the mallet given quite freely, the letter is sunk to the proper depth. Experience and familiarity with the punches obviate this cautionary method.

It will be understood that the letters are cut the right way on the punch, as the impression has to be reversed, so as to come the right way in printing. This is the opposite to printers' type, the letter being cut the reverse way, so that it comes the right way when applied to the paper.

PUNCHING STEMS AND HOOKS.

Although it is possible to have punches for the stems of notes, it is not now usual to punch them, because the stroke of the stem would probably not be uniform in thickness, and the stem has often to be lengthened or shortened. The quaver ties, too, have to be of varying length, and cannot be joined up so perfectly by punching as with the graver.

Some think it is preferable to punch the swells, though they are usually cut. The small slurs are punched, but the larger ones are cut with the lozenge graver, although punches can be obtained for some of them.

In punching brackets, the plate is laid so that the right-hand margin is at the top, and the two extremities of the bracket punch are brought almost up to the two staves which are to be bracketed.

Punches are made for striking the bar lines and ledger lines instead of cutting them, but this is an obsolete practice. All modern engravers cut the bar lines and ledger lines.

Quavers standing alone are usually given a curled hook, for the reason that it is more distinguishable and prints better. Some think it is purely a fanciful way of representing this note, and has no object.

Dots, figures, and expressions are all punched. Punches for such indications as *cresc.*, *dim.*, *rall.*, etc., and for *ff*, *pp*, *mf.*, are obtainable with all the letters on one punch, but these are not much used now, each letter being struck separately. It is difficult to strike the word-punches so as to get the impression even. There are punches for sharps, flats, naturals, and, indeed, every sign used in music.

Figures are punched at the bottom of the plates to indicate the publisher's stock number and the consecutive number of the piece for cataloguing purposes. The name of the publishers is also often added, or their initials, by way of an imprint ; and there is generally a copyright note on the first page of each piece.

THE PLANISHING OR LEVELLING.

After the punching, the plate will be distorted somewhat, and there will be bulges around the notes caused by the metal being forced up by the punches. This must be corrected, before the engraving, by the operation of planishing, which is performed by a special hammer already illustrated. (Fig. 52, Chapter VII.) The plate is laid face up on the anvil, which either rests on the bench, or is mounted on a block of wood resting on the floor. (Figs. 75, 76, 77.) In the latter case, the engraver, whilst seated, grips the block of wood between his knees.

The blows must be struck in such a way that the

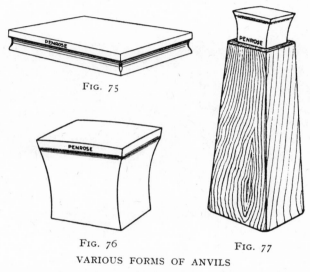

FIG. 75

FIG. 76   FIG. 77

VARIOUS FORMS OF ANVILS

face of the hammer falls flat and squarely on each of the elevations produced by the punch. It is, above all, necessary to avoid producing " half moons " by making a false tap with the edge of the hammer face. This would be by sheer carelessness or inexperience, as the face of the hammer is slightly convex and the anvil face is also a little domed.

To perform the operation properly, the hammer

141

should be held by the end of its handle without stiff-
ness, and it ought to fall and rebound with supple-
ness. The wrist should follow the stroke without
moving the arm. The method of holding the hammer
is illustrated in Fig. 78. The height to which the

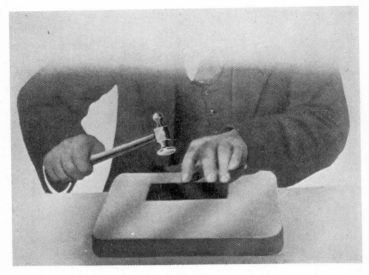

FIG. 78

METHOD OF HOLDING THE LEVELLING HAMMER

hammer should be raised above the plate is important,
and it should not be lifted too high.

Some old engravers pass a steel block over the
surface, hammering with a mallet in the same way as
a printer would plane down a forme of type ; but
modern engravers invariably follow the method we
have outlined.

When plates have taken a curve or are otherwise warped, it is a usual plan to place the plate between two lithographic stones ; but, as a rule, a plate will flatten itself out by its own weight if laid on a stone for a sufficient time.

For large and thick plates, and where the metal is hard, some engravers use a tilt hammer, with a large anvil mounted on a block of wood. The hammer swings in a frame with a pivot near the end of the hammer shaft, and a spring supports the head a little way from the plate, so that the operator has only to press down the hammer with a quick stroke with one hand, whilst moving the plate about on the anvil with the other. No doubt such an arrangement requires some experience in handling, and it is a survival of old-time practice.

It is stated in a publication issued in connection with the Inventions Exhibition of 1885 that the English method is to send the plate to the pewterers to be flattened for printing, whilst the Continental method is for the engravers to flatten their plates themselves. This may have been the case in the early days when the plates contained a larger proportion of tin than now, which made them harder ; and the plates were thicker in the old days, requiring much more effort to flatten them.

One of the old London engravers preserves as a curiosity a hammer for flattening used in the old days. This hammer has a very much heavier head than the flattening hammer now used, being, in fact, more like a cobbler's hammer.

Present-day engravers all flatten their own plates,

and certainly would not care to entrust them to a pewterer.

After the plate has been duly and properly levelled, the engraver proceeds with the cutting. His work would obviously be made more difficult, if not indeed impossible, were the plate not level.

CHAPTER XIII

ENGRAVING AND FINISHING

THE operation of engraving is performed in the same way as engraving a copper plate, except that, instead of the plate resting on a sandbag or a small desk, it is laid flat on the bench, which is usually covered with a millboard or leather board, the smoothness of the surface in either case facilitating the turning of the plate. It must be turned in different directions to get the best angle for cutting, so that the tool point is always thrust forward from right to left. The method of holding and using the graver must be learnt by the beginner. It is grasped firmly in the right hand with the handle in the hollow of the palm, the little finger being pressed against the side of the handle in the narrow part if pear shape, or in the hollow under the handle if mushroom shape. The little finger thus keeps the tool steady in the hollow of the hand without assistance from the other fingers or the thumb. To get the correct position for the other fingers, the tool, still held by the little finger, is rested on the plate with the underside of the blade and handle touching. The handle is then raised slightly so that the point only is resting on the surface. The first finger and thumb are now pressed against the sides of the blade so as to prevent the tool leaning over sideways—in either direction. The thumb should rest firmly on the plate, the graver being pushed forward so as to slide against the ball of the thumb, which thus steadies the hand upon the plate; whilst the first finger presses the blade against the thumb, and also

FIG. 79

THE CORRECT WAY TO HOLD THE GRAVER

forces the point of the tool into the plate. The other two fingers do practically nothing but help to hold the tool in the most convenient way. The wrist also plays an important part, but the engraver is not conscious of it when engraving any more than a writer is when using the pen. We give an illustration showing how the graver is held (Fig. 79), but the beginner will do better if he can get an expert engraver to show him the right way. One of the most experienced engravers says the right way to hold a graver is as a violinist would hold his bow, but that depends perhaps on the shape of the handle.

FIG. 80

POSITION WHEN CUTTING WITH THE GRAVER

The tool is pushed with the forearm parallel to the plate, and the palm of the hand pushing the tool forward against the guidance of the thumb. There must be no tendency to raise the handle, as this would depress the point and make it dig too deeply into the metal. An exception is in cutting ledger lines, when it is necessary to raise the handle slightly. Fig. 80 shows the position whilst a line is being cut.

The bar lines, stems of the notes, the ledger lines the ties of the quavers, the swells and slurs, are the only parts, as a rule, that are cut, unless there are some unusual signs for which no punches are available. The bar lines are cut first, then the stems, ledger lines, and ties, and, lastly, the slurs and swells.

The bars may be cut with a graver, but are more often cut with a single point score tool described in Chapter VII (Fig. 45), this being guided by the T-square, with its head laid against the top of the plate. The double lines at the end of a section or piece are cut either with two strokes of the single tool, or with a double-pointed tool which makes the cut at one stroke, one point making a fine line and the other a thick one. This is not always so, however, the lines being often of the same thickness. The rule as to this is controlled by musical law.

The ledger lines are cut with a fine flat scorper, following the scratch made in the pointing of the plate.

The stems of the notes are cut with the tint graver. (Chapter VII, Fig. 57.) The stems should have a length equal to three spaces of the score tool, except in the case of the stems of connected quavers, which ought to reach to the ties of the notes.

The ties are cut with scorpers, which have a flat back. (Chapter VII, Fig. 60.) These vary in thickness according to the width to be cut, this naturally depending on the size of the notes. The tool is given a slight oscillatory movement by a turn of the wrist.

148

This aids the tool in cutting and gives to the bottom of the cut a waviness which helps to retain the printing ink.

In the case of double or triple hooks, it is necessary to make the strokes perfectly parallel and fairly close together. There is no hard-and-fast rule for sloping the hooks of connected notes. They follow the general trend of the pitch of the notes.

The large slurs are usually cut with the lozenge graver. Small slurs are, however, generally punched.

It is necessary in cutting a slur with the graver to begin finely, pushing the blade first whilst it is held level, then inclining it little by little, so that the cheeks of the tool sink more and more deeply into the metal, thus forming the thick part of the stroke, and, finally, levelling the blade again, so as to finish with the same fineness as at the beginning of the cut.

When commencing the cutting of a slur, it is found a good plan to indicate with the drawing point the exact curve, in order to guide the graver. For the sake of good appearance, the slurs must not be too much arched.

The " swells " are cut with the single-pointed score tool against the edge of the T-square, if they are large, and, if small, with the elliptical graver.

The ends of the staves, if they have not finished quite up to the bar lines, should be finished with a tint graver. (Chapter VII, Fig. 57.)

The cutting being finished, it is necessary to pass the score tool again through the staves, in order to open the lines which have been closed up by the punching, especially near the chords, minims, semi-breves, and accidentals which are on the lines. Care should be taken in using the score tool in this way, because the teeth of the tool, in passing over the hollows caused by the punching, may easily jump out of the lines. It is for this reason perhaps that some engravers prefer to use the graver known as the " Trotter," but others hold that it is quite unnecessary to use this tool for such a purpose.

The plate is examined in detail to see if there is any touching up to do, or any faulty signs to re-punch. If the stem of a note is of insufficient length, either not touching the note or not joining the hook in case of a quaver, this must be remedied by a touch of the graver.

By means of the burnisher, all useless dots or lines are effaced. It is necessary to see that no scratch or pit is left on the surface, as these would hold the ink and show up in the printing. (Fig. 81.)

As the edges of the engraved lines have a burr on each side, it is necessary to remove this with the scraper, which should be lightly drawn diagonally across the cut lines, passing over the whole plate until all is smooth and level.

CORRECTIONS.

It is one of the great advantages of engraving on pewter plates that corrections can be easily made. The usual course before the proof goes to the composer, is for the " reader," employed in all large establishments, to mark off the errors which are deviations from the manuscript. The engraver then proceeds to mark on the back of the plate the places corresponding to the signs to be corrected. For that purpose, he uses the correcting callipers. (Fig. 50, Chapter VII.)

The plate is passed between the two legs of the callipers, bringing the point of the top leg down on

FIG. 81

METHOD OF USING THE BURNISHER

the sign to be corrected, then pressing the point down whilst the plate rests partly on the edge of the bench. The point of the other leg underneath the plate is pressed on the back so as to indicate the exact place for making the correction. Usually the point is made to draw a cross or circle to more legibly indicate the place than would be done by only pressing the point into the metal. In the same way, all other corrections to be done are indicated. The plate is then laid face down on the stone and the places indicated are punched with a medium size dot punch. Generally four dots are punched, so as to raise four bumps on the surface inside the note. It is necessary to stamp sufficiently deep to force up the metal, and the dots must follow the form of the note. Then the plate is turned over and, with the aid of the burnisher, the raised parts corresponding to the dots

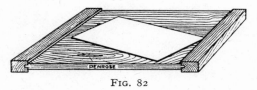

FIG. 82

SCRAPING BOARD

are rubbed together until the old work is obliterated and the surface made fairly smooth. The back is also gently tapped with the correcting hammer to remove any burr created by the dots. It is necessary to avoid striking beyond the part where the sign is to be effaced, or the neighbouring signs or notes may be deformed.

After the burnishing, the triangular scraper is used. The engraver localizes the position of the scraper so as to find a place on the curve of its cutting edge which will suit the size of the area to be scraped ; then he gently scrapes away until the plate assumes its virgin appearance in the part operated upon. The necessary rectification is now made, the score

152

lines being joined up, and the punching and engraving done as originally.

If the corrections cover a comparatively large area, the portion affected is scraped down with the " busk," which is held bent to a curve so as to localize the correction. This way of correcting requires great care, as it creates a hollow, entailing a lot of pushing of the metal from the back.

The scraping board, which is used by some engravers in conjunction with the " busk," is here illustrated. (Fig. 82.)

Another method of correcting is that known as " blowing-out." This is done with the blowpipe, and in skilful hands is quite successful.

After the correcting, the triangular scraper is applied over the whole plate to make it level and neat.

The composer's alterations receive the same treatment when the proofs are returned, and a second proof is usually sent.

CHAPTER XIV

PROOFING, TRANSFERRING, AND PRINTING

IT was formerly the custom to " pull " proofs in the copperplate manner on the copperplate printer's press. This method consists of smearing the plate with ink in such a way as to work it well into the lines of the engraving ; wiping the surface ; laying a piece of damped paper on it, backed with a blanket ; and pulling the whole through the press. This is a very perfect method of printing, which will give the best results from the plate for high-class printed copies ; but for proofs the objection was raised that the results showed a totally different effect to that which would be obtained finally in the lithographic printing, as the lines and notes appeared too sharp and thin.

It has now become the practice for music engravers to " pull " proofs by simply inking the surface of the plate with a composition roller, as used by letterpress printers, charged with a blue or green ink. In this way only the surface is inked and printed from, so that the engraved parts show white on a dark ground. The reason for using the blue or green ink is that it is easy to see any corrections marked in black ink on the proof. These prints are sometimes called " magic-lantern proofs," in allusion to their similarity to a lantern slide when looked at by transmitted light.

At first an objection was raised to these proofs, but they have now become popular, and those who have to read them for corrections say they are more restful to the eye than an ordinary black-and-white proof would be. It has, in fact, been seriously proposed to print all music in this way. The lithographic printers, it is said, do not like these proofs, because the quality of the plate is shown too well and the imperfections of their own work are too clearly revealed.

As the engraver may be called upon to print the ordinary proofs in black lines on white paper, it will be well, for the benefit of those who are unacquainted with plate printing, to describe the method.

The copperplate press (Fig. 83) is usually and preferably employed ; but a lithographer would be able to " pull " proofs on his lithographic hand-press, in which the pressure is applied by means of a leather-covered scraper, acting like a squeegee. The small presses used by artists for proofing etchings will also serve the purpose of proofing music plates, though these presses have a tendency to curve the plates owing to the small diameter of the cylinders. For experimental purposes a household wringer with rubber rollers may be used as a makeshift.

The ink may be purchased ready for use, but some engravers prefer to make their own ink. This may be done in the following manner : A sufficient amount of lampblack is taken, perhaps four or five table-spoonsful, and spread in the form of a ring on the ink slab, which is usually an old lithographic stone. In the centre of this ring a little medium strength

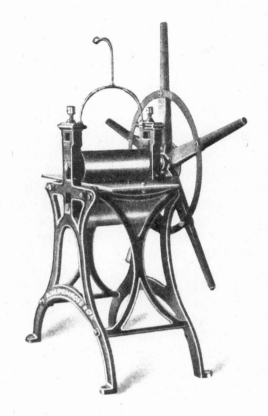

FIG. 83

COPPERPLATE PRESS

copperplate oil is poured, and the black is mixed into it with a palette knife, until the whole is made into a paste of such consistency that it will not run. A muller (Fig. 84) of marble, glass, zinc, or wood is used to grind the black down to the desired fineness, if it has a tendency to be gritty. A few drops of strong copperplate oil is finally added for the purpose of making the ink adhere well to the plate and paper.

A dabber (Fig. 85) or a felt roller, charged with this ink, is worked over the whole surface of the plate. If the dabber is used, it is rocked in such a way that the ink is worked well into the lines until the engraving is quite filled.

To clean off the surplus ink from the surface, some engravers use a long palette knife, which has a straight smooth edge, using it as a scraper, but this requires some skill to get a clean wipe and to avoid scratching the plate. A piece of " doctor " blade, as used by calico and wallpaper printers for wiping their printing cylinders, would be an improvement on the palette knife for this purpose. It consists of a very flexible steel strip about $2\frac{1}{2}$ in. broad, and with a perfectly straight and smooth edge filed off to about 45 degrees. It is trailed over the plate with the bevelled edge under at an angle which is found by experience to give the best results. It should not be pushed against its edge. It is all the better if given a shearing motion to avoid streaks. The blade is best clipped in a wooden holder, as used by cabinet-makers for scraping wood. (Fig. 86.) It may be found best, with this method of wiping, to use the ink thinner.

The danger of scratching the plate by using the palette knife for wiping has led many printers to adopt the plan of using pieces of pressboard. This is a very stiff, highly glazed cardboard, which can be cut with a clean edge. The pieces are cut up to about $1\frac{1}{2} \times 1\frac{1}{4}$ in., one of these being taken between

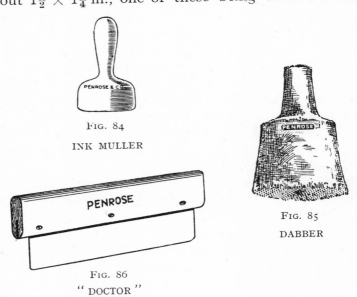

FIG. 84

INK MULLER

FIG. 85

DABBER

FIG. 86

" DOCTOR "

the thumb and fingers and dragged across the plate in a direction about 60 degrees to the stave lines, whilst held sloping in the direction it is being drawn. The plate is, of course, inked in the cold state with comparatively thin ink, so that it is easy to wipe in this way ; whereas it would be impossible with the stiff ink which is used for copperplate printing, and which requires that the plate should be heated to assist the wiping.

After scraping away as much as possible of the ink in this way, getting the plate as clean as is practicable, a rag soaked in a weak solution of caustic soda or potash, and well wrung out so that it is just damp, is passed lightly over the plate, followed by another. This is succeeded by another rag, which must be absolutely clean, so that no trace of ink is left on the surface. The rag used is that known as meat cloth, but copperplate printers use muslin followed by a coarse hemp net. A final polish with the palm of the hand, on which whitening is rubbed, is given to copper plates, and might perhaps be used to advantage on music plates if done skilfully

The paper used for proofing in this manner may be a thin common printing paper, such as is used for newspapers ; but, more generally, a thin soft-sized wove paper, having an appearance like Manila paper, is used. It should previously be damped by being left for some minutes under several thicknesses of damp blotting or plate paper, in the same way as the lithographer damps his transfer paper.

It only remains now to lay the sheet of damped paper on to the surface of the plate, covering it with the usual blankets used by plate printers (known as " fronting " and " backing "), and a pressboard over these, then pulling through the press. On lifting the proof from the plate, the ink should entirely leave the lines and stand in relief on the paper, which will have a glazed appearance, due to the pressure and contact with the polished surface of the plate.

For printing an edition direct from the plate, better paper should, of course, be used, and more care taken in the inking and wiping. The plates ought to be thicker and harder than for transfer work, the edges and corners being rounded off to prevent the paper being cut through. Direct printing is, however, seldom done, except for a limited *edition de luxe*.

TRANSFERS.

For pulling transfers for lithography, the ink used should be of a special character. Such transfer ink may be bought ready-prepared, but experienced printers usually make their own. It consists of a variety of ingredients, such as soap, fat, wax, and lampblack, and it is usually made in hard wedge-shaped sticks, so that it may be conveniently held in the hand. Practically it is the same as copperplate transfer ink. Being hard, it has to be softened by warming the plate on a copperplate heater (Fig. 87). This is heated by an atmospheric gas burner, but we have heard of plates being heated by steam introduced into copper tubes, flattened so as to give increased heating surface and placed about 2 in. apart. An electric heater could also be used.

The first step is to see the plate is thoroughly cleaned from any remains of old ink in the lines, if it has been previously used. The ink in such case should be brushed out with turpentine. Then the plate is placed on the heater and warmed up until it will melt the stick of ink applied to it. The surface is rubbed all over with the ink. Next, a piece of wood formed with a straight edge and covered with leather, is pushed to and fro over the plate, in the same manner as a squeegee is used, so as to force the ink into the lines. The surplus ink is next wiped off with pieces of pressboard (if that way of wiping is adopted), as already described, or with a sweep of the palette knife or " doctor." A soft cotton cloth is then taken and made up into a pad, with which the plate is lightly wiped. This is followed by another pad moistened with a few drops of potash or soda

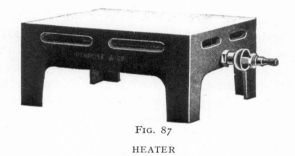

FIG. 87

HEATER

lye. The scum left after this wiping will still be considerable, and will show itself as a tint on the paper. If the impression was pulled on lithographic transfer paper, this scum would give much trouble when the transfer to stone was made ; but the music transfer being on plain paper, the scum is to a large extent absorbed into the surface, and thus gives no trouble in transferring.

The German method of pulling transfers is slightly different to the English one. The ink is in the form of a cylindrical stick, and is generally enclosed in some fabric, except at the end which is put into contact with the plate. The plate is heated and the stick of ink rubbed over its surface. Twill rag is used for the wiping after most of the surplus ink has been removed by pieces of shalloon board (the pressboard already referred to). The second cleaning is done with pearlash or potash solutions applied to the pad, and a final wipe with whitening is applied with the palm of the hand. India paper is generally used for pulling the transfers upon, and it is damped immediately before laying in position on the plate. When re-transferring to the stone or zinc for printing, the back of the paper is damped with a sponge just prior to laying down. This is considered preferable to using the damping-book, as in that case the damping might not be uniform in the case of work patched up with corrections, and a good joining up of the staves with the patched portion would not be obtained.

The author is indebted to Mr. Joseph Goodman, the well-known authority on lithography, for this account of the German method, which he saw employed in the Röder music printing works. He gives a full account of what he saw on his visit there in an article in the *Modern Lithographer* (Vol. IV, 1908, p. 151) under the title of " The Largest Music Printers in the World."

Usually there will be sufficient ink left on the transfer paper to lay down the work with one pull through the press, though sometimes the plate is turned round and pulled through again. Occasionally it is necessary to take off a little of the excess of ink on the transfer by pulling it through the press with light pressure in contact with a sheet of paper,

162

because if the ink stands up too much in relief on the transfer, it may " squash " and give a blurred impression.

The lithographic method of transferring to the stone or printing plate is well known to most printers and engravers ; but for the benefit of those who are unfamiliar with the operation, we will describe it.

Whilst the stone or plate is being got ready on the press, the transfers are placed in the damping book, which consists of about a quire of thick plate paper which has been uniformly damped through and placed between two wooden boards. A sheet of thin paper is placed against the face of the transfer to prevent excess of moisture reaching the surface.

If corrections or additions have to be made, they are done beforehand by patching-up, either by pasting on pieces of transfer paper bearing the corrections, or by pricking the paper at the corners with needles. This latter way has the effect of anchoring the patch to the main transfer sufficiently to allow of its being laid down. It is also adopted in preference to using paste, which might cause the transfer to cockle, for attaching several transfers to one sheet when laying down several pages at a time. The sheet to which they are attached is prepared with a varnished surface that remains tacky. The position for the pages is marked on the sheet, and the transfers with their margins carefully trimmed to squareness are laid to the marks ; then the corners and margins are pricked with a needle point to make them adhere. In this way, a large sheet of eight or more pages can be laid down at once.

If the transfer is made to lithographic stone, the latter is ground quite flat and carefully polished. It is laid on the bed of the lithographic press and carefully levelled up, if found to be out of parallelism, with the scraper. Guide marks for laying on the transfer sheet are made with a piece of printer's " lead," and the sheet is laid carefully to these marks. Backing sheets of paper, blanket, and pressboard are laid over the transfer, the zinc-covered tympan brought down over the whole, and the bed supporting the stone is run through the press several times with gradually increased pressure applied to the scraper by means of the adjusting screw. Fig. 88 shows the usual form of lithographic press.

Should the transfer have to be made to zinc or aluminium, the sheet of metal is given a finely ground surface by grinding with sand and marbles in the tray of a graining machine, which keeps the marbles in constant motion over the surface. Some chemical treatment is also given, and the plate, after being washed and dried off, is laid on a stone or on an iron bed resting on the bed of the press. The operations of laying down the transfer and pulling through the press are the same as for stone.

After the paper backing of the transfer has been removed, the stone or metal surface is sponged first with clean water and then with gum solution, and allowed to dry. When the surface is damped again, the gum has the property of holding the moisture, which prevents the ink from adhering to the bare parts of the surface. The ink on the leather roller, which is applied to the printing surface, then refreshes

164

and builds up the ink from the transfer until a sufficient amount is obtained on the lines to enable them to be printed. The first layer of ink is usually washed off with a special solution, which removes the ink from the surface without destroying the greasy

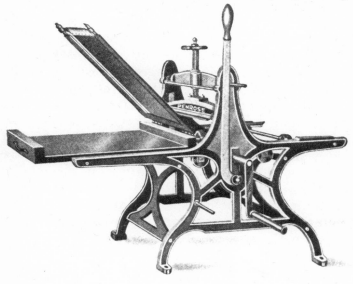

Fig 88

LITHOGRAPHIC PRESS

image which has penetrated the stone or metal plate. The inking-up is repeated, and the ink from the roller is then taken up by the lines of the image. Finally, the work is given an " etch " with an acid solution, which sharpens up the lines and cleans the bare surface, so as to make the work roll up better in the subsequent operations of printing.

Invariably, more cleaning up has to be done for music work than for copperplate transfers, on account of the susceptibility of the pewter plates to scratches and other faults which hold the ink.

The reason why zinc and aluminium have been used in recent years in place of stone for lithography is chiefly on account of the facility with which the plates may be bent round the cylinder of a rotary zincographic printing machine or an offset press. For such purposes, the music pages are usually transferred first to stone, from which re-transfers are pulled for transfer to the metal plates. The reason for this is that the stone offers greater facility for cleaning up and getting the work into good condition than does metal. Usually, 4, 8, 12, or 16 pages are put down on the plate for printing on one sheet. The printing follows the ordinary course of lithographic work, the machine performing automatically the operations of inking, damping, and impressing the image on the paper.

OFFSET PRINTING.

The " offset " method of printing consists in first making the impression on a rubber-covered cylinder, which, in turn, transfers or " offsets " the print on to paper. The advantage is that on rough surfaced or dull matt paper a sharper and more pleasing impression is obtained than from direct printing (plate to paper). The latter method requires for obtaining the best effects a smooth paper, which is not liked by musicians, because its shininess makes the music difficult to read. If a dull-surfaced paper is used, the printing may be thick and somewhat blurred.

TITLE-PAGES.

The ordinary title-page in black is printed at the same time as the music pages, but coloured titles are printed at a separate operation, sometimes entailing several printings. The back page of advertisements is sometimes printed with the title-page. In this case, the black printing is usually the last, and forms the " key " or outline printing for the coloured cover.

A few old pieces are sometimes found with a Baxter print pasted on the cover, and these are eagerly sought after by collectors. Baxter was a famous colour printer, whose work was usually printed from woodcuts.

Title-pages are made up from all forms of litho-graphic work—line, crayon, " splash," air brush, half-tone, and by means of shading mediums. These latter consist of gelatine films with lines, dots, or patterns in relief. The films are inked and trans-ferred to parts of the drawing where they can be appropriately applied. For gold printing, the part required in gold is printed in a varnish ink and, whilst still wet, bronze powder is brushed over, so that it adheres.

CHAPTER XV

TYPOGRAPHICALLY-PRINTED MUSIC

AS indicated in our historical chapters, attempts have been made from the earliest times to print music typographically, and the method is, indeed, the oldest of all ways of music printing. The tendency, however, has always been towards an increased production of engraved music. Typographically-printed music has never, in fact, been popular for sheet music, albums, orchestral scores, band parts, and complicated instrumental works. The reasons for this preference are not altogether due to fashion or fancy, but to the fact that lithographed music, whether from transfers or from engraved plates, is thought to be clearer and more easy to read, especially where the notes are crowded, the rhythm irregular, or the parts interwoven. Another advantage is that the spacing between the engraved notes, signs, etc., can be more minutely graduated to suit the sense of expression of the passage. Litho printing has, in fact, a more musicianly appearance ; it is a kind of pictorial representation of the composition. A further point in regard to appearance is that there are no minute breaks in the lines, the tails of the notes, etc., such as occur in type-set music, especially when the type becomes worn.

A more practical reason for the popularity of the

engraved and lithographed music is its simplicity, speed, and cheapness in production, which makes it very suitable for the printing of small editions.

The largely increased cost of printing since the war has had its effect on typographic music printing, and has led many publishers who have hitherto used it to turn their attention to engraved music.

In spite of the drawbacks we have mentioned, letterpress music is being more largely used now than at any preceding period. It is largely used for collections of hymn tunes, songs, anthems, Church services, cantatas, oratorios, musical periodicals, supplements to journals, instruction books, etc.

The advantages of typographic music are that it can be printed along with ordinary letterpress and illustrations in the text pages of books, newspapers, and periodicals ; it can, moreover, be printed with the same speed and at the same cost.

Lithographic printing is relatively slower and dearer, though music publishers think that this is balanced by the cheaper production of the engraved plates compared with typesetting. Such comparisons as the latter, however, are beside the mark, for the fact is that letterpress printing has its own particular field, and could not be displaced by lithographed music for such purposes as we have indicated.

It is undeniable that the setting up of music type is a difficult and tedious operation, and there seems to be no way of simplifying it. A large number of separate pieces of type have to be used. For instance, a bar of eight consecutive notes in $\frac{3}{4}$ time, and with a tenor clef, contains at least seventy-eight characters, and there will be more if the measure contains accidentals or complicated harmony.

Even the blank spaces between the notes represent five or more separate pieces of type ; but when the music has long runs from the top to the bottom of the keyboard, as in Paderewski's " Minuet," the composition is made extremely difficult, for all the ledger lines above and below the staves have to be embedded in a mass of quads and spaces, so that the notes may not be displaced in handling the forme, in taking proofs, and in printing.

The more ornamental or brilliant a piece of music, the more complicated it is to set in type, because all the slurs and other expression marks have to be fitted between the notes. Music of such a character is accordingly best engraved and printed lithographically.

It is obvious that no ordinary compositor can proceed to set up music type until he has gained some experience of the work. It is essential that he should have some knowledge of music, otherwise he will inevitably make mistakes without knowing he has done so. As a matter of fact, most music compositors have a good knowledge of music, and many of them are expert musicians, fulfilling professional engagements in their spare time.

It has been stated that four or five years are necessary for training apprentices in setting music type, and even after that they are learning and improving by practice every day so long as they are in the business.

So far as we are able to gather, the work is not taught in any of the technical schools in this country. Thus there is little or no encouragement to the training of apprentices, and it will be found that in printing offices where music typesetting is done, it is in the hands of comparatively old men.

There is little information to be gained on the subject from published works, if we except two pamphlets in the German language. One is by Robert Dittrich, published at Leipzig by Alexander Waldrow, in 1872, entitled *Anleitung zum Satz der Musiknoten-typen* (Directions for the Setting of Music Type). This gives full instructions, showing the separate type characters, and giving the lay of the case. The other is by J. H. Bachmann, published in 1875, also at Leipzig, by the same publishers, and entitled *Die Schule des Musiknoten Satzes* (The School of Music Typesetting). This is arranged on much the same lines as the former, and is more complete. There is also a small pamphlet, in French, entitled *Manuel de Typographie Musical* by Theophile Beaudoir, Paris.

In the English language, the reader will find a chapter on setting music type in John Southward's book *Modern Practical Printing*. The lay of the case is there illustrated and a number of practical hints are given.

The American publication, *The Inland Printer*, in 1898–99, gave a series of articles by W. H. Driffield on music typesetting.

These books may be consulted in the Blades' Library at the St. Bride's Foundation Institute.

171

Southward's book is a current work which may be purchased.

A good deal of preliminary information can be obtained from a study of typefounders' specimen books, and from the synopsis sheets showing the separate characters. On these latter sheets, every character is shown separately, and is numbered to facilitate the ordering of extra " sorts." The typefounders also issue sheets showing suggestions for the " lay " of the cases.

Messrs. P. M. Shanks & Sons, Ltd., an old-established firm formerly known as the Patent Type-founding Co., Ltd., have for many years specialized in music typefounding. This firm issued a specimen sheet in 1863 showing three sizes of music type, described as Ruby No. 3, Diamond No. 3, and Semi-Nonpareil No. 4.

It is interesting to compare the prices of music type at that time with those ruling now, or rather with the pre-war prices which are given on the specimen sheets. On the 1863 specimen sheet the prices were : Ruby No. 3, 5s. 8d. per lb. ; Diamond No. 3, 7s. 9d. per lb. ; Semi-Nonpareil No. 4, 14s. 6d. per lb. for founts of 60 lbs. and upwards. The firm show in their present-day specimen sheets six kinds of music type, viz., Semi-Nonpareil No. 4, 28s. per lb. ; Gem, 18s. 8d. per lb ; Diamond Nos. 2, 3, and 5, 14s. 2d. per lb. ; and Ruby No. 3, 12s. per lb. The numbers after the names of the founts do not indicate different sizes, but varying shapes of the heads of the notes.

The most used founts are the Gem and Diamond,

GEM MUSIC.

FIG. 89

SPECIMEN OF GEM MUSIC TYPE, BY P. M. SHANKS AND SONS, LTD.

but there is a steady demand for the Semi-Nonpareil, which is used for small hymn-books. For certain sizes of page, it is found that more notes can be got on a page by using Semi-Nonpareil or Gem instead of the Diamond, though the latter is a more readable size.

Messrs. R. H. Stevens & Co., of Southwark Street, S.E., who are the successors of Messrs. V. & J. Figgins, a very old London firm of typefounders, also offer a very good selection of music founts. Their sizes are Brilliant, Gem, Diamond, Ruby, Pearl No. 2, and Nonpareil No. 2. They also supply what is termed " Short Score " founts in the above sizes.

Messrs. Miller & Richard, Edinburgh, another very old-established typefounding firm, have been casting music type for over sixty years. They show three sizes on their specimen sheet, viz., Ruby, Pearl, Diamond and Gem.

Each of these firms also supply several sizes for Tonic Sol-Fa music, to which we refer in a later chapter.

Messrs. Shanks and Messrs. Stevens issue founts for the Gregorian or chant music, which we deal with in another chapter.

There is one feature about the sizes of music type which will be of particular interest to printers, viz., that music type is not definitely cast on the " point " system. The reason is that music type was standardized many years before this system came into use, and it would not pay to reorganize all the type-casting mechanism when there is such a comparatively limited demand for music type. It may be

174

DIAMOND SHORT SCORE.

FIG. 90

SPECIMEN OF DIAMOND SHORT SCORE MUSIC TYPE, BY R. H. STEVENS AND CO.

PEARL-DIAMOND.

Hear my Prayer, O Lord.

Hear my pray'r, hear my pray'r, O Lord, give ear, give ear, to my pray'r

FIG. 91

SPECIMEN OF MILLER AND RICHARDS' PEARL-DIAMOND MUSIC TYPE

175

said that music type has a " point " system of its
own, otherwise it would be impossible to get the
various pieces of type to line up. It is true of
Shanks's Semi-Nonpareil to say that it is 3-point,
but the other sizes are not on point bodies, nor to the
Standard Line system. The Gem, for instance, will
not line up if the pieces are reversed. Even if the
point and standard line systems were adopted for
music type, it would be extremely inconvenient for
those who already have a stock of music type to
adopt the new system. Further, there would be no
advantage in the conversion, as the music type
characters are not required to line up with the textual
type characters. No inconvenience is caused, so far
as we can learn, through this lack of the point system ;
typefounders interchange music founts with one
another and, therefore, all adopt the same standards.

The names adopted for music founts are those
prevailing for type sizes before the point system came
into use, and these names are well known to printers.
It may be useful to point out for the benefit of the
younger members of the printing craft that the Semi-
Nonpareil, as its name implies, is cast on a half nonpareil or 3-point body ; the Gem is on half brevier,
the Diamond is half bourgeois, and the Ruby is
practically (though not exactly) half small pica.

A printer proposing to order a fount of music type
may require to know what weight he should order.
Naturally, the size of the type must be considered,
the smaller sizes yielding more characters to the
pound. The weight of a minimum fount usually
advised by the typefounders is 60 lbs., this being

176

just sufficient to fill an upper and lower case. No objection would be raised to supplying a fount of 30 lbs., but it would be regarded as in the nature of an amateur outfit. Of course, a music printing firm doing work on a large scale would order much more than 60 lbs. of one size. One large firm of music printers has ordered founts of 500 lbs. at a time and, even then, had to frequently order extra sorts. Another firm which had a fount of Gem size, weighing 2,000 lbs., bought it when the price was 6s. 6d. per lb. ; it is now 18s. 8d. per lb.

The practice, mentioned in another chapter, of stereotyping or electrotyping after a page or two is set, and then distributing the type, would obviously be inconvenient for working on anything like a commercial scale. Besides, the type would suffer greater wear and tear in this way, especially if the electrotyper or stereotyper was not used to dealing with music type. It is probably due to bad stereotyping more than anything else that typographically-printed music has been brought into disrepute.

There is some variance between different authorities as to the number of " sorts," i.e. separate pieces or characters in a fount of music type. Dittrich, the German author already referred to, shows 365 boxes in his diagram of the case, whilst Bachmann shows 302. Driffield gives 371, but says that to these must be added nine different sizes of quads, two or three of which may be contained in the same box, making 380 different pieces. There are, he says, no less than twenty-eight different characters for various combinations of the black notes, whilst the five lines of the stave which appear so even and exact when printed are made up of many pieces. Another authority says that every character is now represented by one or more pieces and, in addition, there are many sorts essential to correct justification, making in all between 300 and 400 characters in a complete music fount.

Probably about 400 may be taken as a fair average of the number of useful sorts. The best evidence, however, as to the number of sorts is afforded by the typefounders' synopsis sheets, one of which we reproduce. (Fig. 92.) Messrs. Shanks show 487 separate characters, including spaces and quads, on their sheet of Diamond type, and 464 on their sheet of Gem ; but this does not represent all, as customers often order special sorts which raise the total to 500 or more. Messrs. Stevens give 451 characters on their synopsis sheet for Diamond music type, and they also supply special characters when required.

Messrs. Clowes, the well-known printers, who cast themselves a good deal of the music type they use, say that their founts run to about 460 characters.

The difference in the number of sorts in a fount is accounted for by the inclusion of new characters, and also by casting logotypes of such expressions as *cres.* and *dim.* In the Diamond size, pieces are also cast with two lines on a double body for building up staves, and some of the note heads have part of the stave lines attached to them to facilitate joining up.

It may be thought by those who are inexperienced in music typesetting that it would be better to have pieces of the stave, consisting of five lines, cast in

178

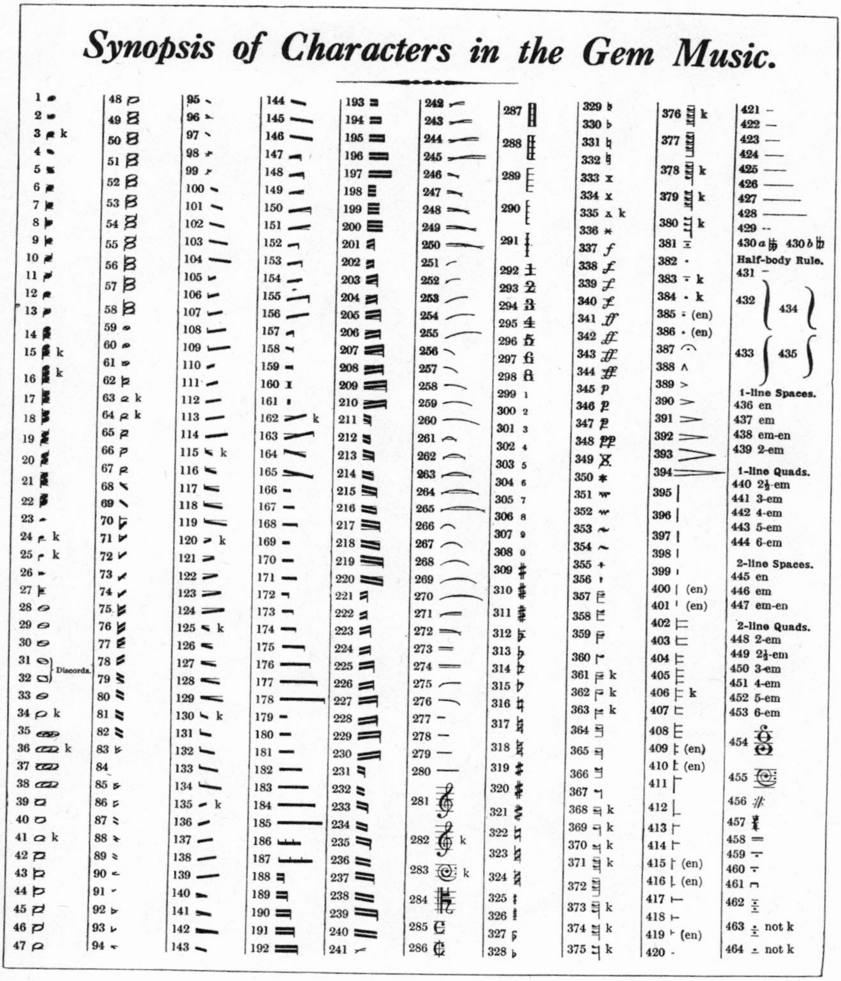

Synopsis of Characters in the Gem Music.

FIG. 92

SYNOPSIS SHEET OF CHARACTERS IN SHANKS' MUSIC TYPE

(2370) bet. pp. 178 and 179

one block for parts where there are no notes. Some typefounders, notably Messrs. Stevens, do cast three-, four-, and five-line pieces ; but, in practice, it is said to be best to build up with separate pieces for each line, as there would be a risk of the large pieces getting their corners or the ends of the lines battered, so that the whole would have to be thrown away. Under the present system, a batter may only affect one small piece, and this is an important consideration, for music type being relatively more expensive than ordinary type, the sorts are more costly to replace.

Ordinary brass rules are used at the beginning of staves, and compositors often make up expression marks, such as the *crescendo* and *diminuendo*, or slurs, by means of brass rules, when these signs are extra long.

One thing which determines the number of " sorts " required is the character of the music to be printed, whether vocal or instrumental, the latter requiring more sorts than the former.

The words of songs or hymns are set in ordinary type of a size suitable to that of the music type employed.

There seems to be no definite standard as to the size of music type cases (the trays for holding the type), nor as to the arrangement of the boxes in them. The German cases are constructed especially for holding music type, and are of a much larger size than the ordinary English type cases. Dittrich gives a size which, when translated into English measurements, is 45 × 28 in., and having 365 boxes. Bachmann illustrates a somewhat similar case, which is 48 × 27 in., with 302 boxes. The depth of the boxes in both cases is $1\frac{3}{8}$ in.

179

English printers do not seem to favour such special cases. An objection to them is that they would be inconvenient to use in the ordinary composing frames or racks. The general practice is to use ordinary type cases and, if a pair of cases is not sufficient, the less used sorts are kept in an additional case in the rack under the frame.

Where two compositors work side by side, it is sometimes the practice to place between their cases a pair of narrow cases in which are contained the least-used " sorts." Each man can then draw on these intermediate cases.

Southward, in his book *Modern Printing*, shows an ordinary treble case for the upper and a double case for the lower one, the pair holding 252 " sorts." This is stated to be suitable for Miller & Richards's Gem type. As, however, there are 464 characters in this fount, it is obvious that at least another case would have to be employed for the remaining " sorts."

Messrs. Shanks sell two sizes of cases specially constructed for music type. One pair is recommended as suitable for Semi-Nonpareil, Diamond, and Ruby, and measures $36 \times 14\frac{1}{2}$ in., which is the ordinary English type case size, the pair containing 295 boxes. The other is a special size ($37\frac{1}{2} \times 15$ in.), which is too large for the top of the usual frame ; there are 440 boxes in the pair. These latter cases are evidently based on the design of the ordinary treble upper and lower cases, but an additional number of boxes is obtained by dividing some of the boxes diagonally and otherwise. The compositors often improvise these diagonal divisions by fitting

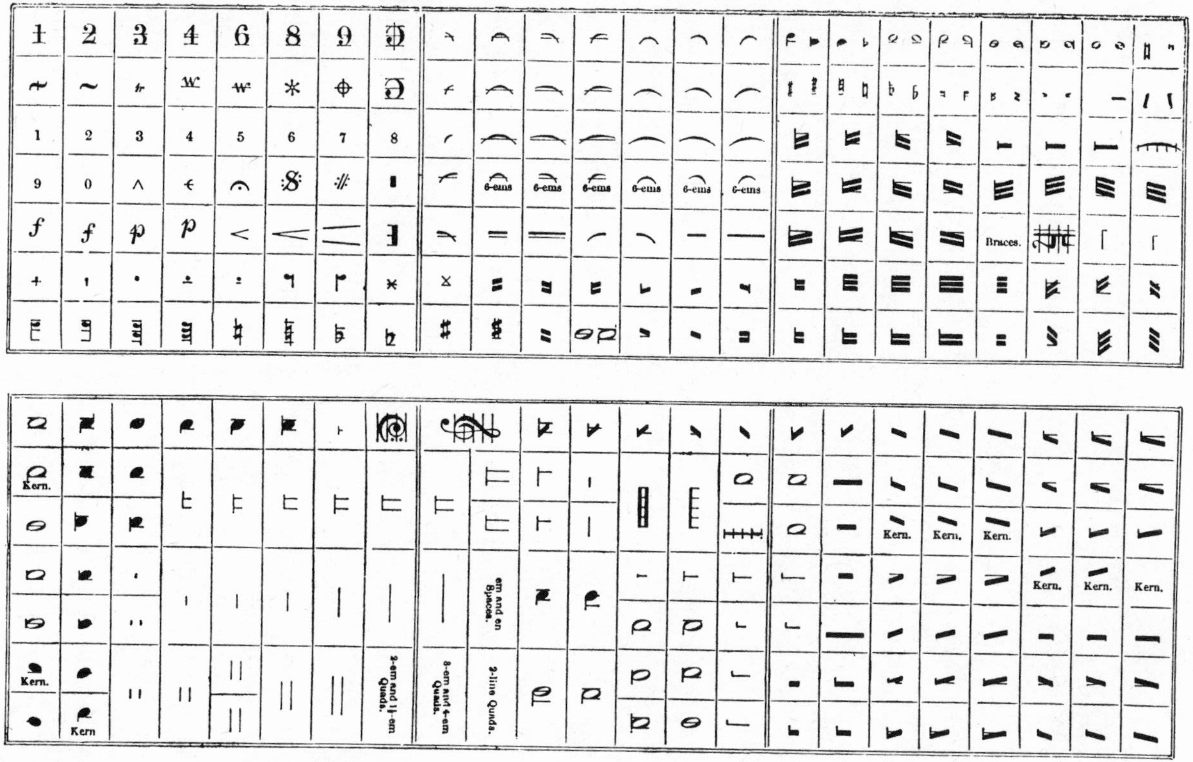

FIG. 93

SUGGESTED PLAN OF MUSIC CASES, BY P. M. SHANKS AND SONS, LTD.

in pieces of brass rule. We give a diagram showing one of the styles of cases employed. (Fig. 93.)

Whilst in most of the boxes the type is laid like ordinary type, it is often the practice to stand some " sorts " on their feet in the upper case, so that the compositor can readily see the face and more quickly pick up the required character.

Whatever form of cases are employed, a suitable " lay " must be determined upon, unless the type-founders' plan is adopted. For the benefit of the uninitiated in typographic matters, the " lay " of the case may be explained as the system on which the various types are located in their boxes or compartments of the cases. The prevailing idea in planning a " lay " is that the more used " sorts " are nearest the hand, and are contained in the largest boxes. The compositor, once he has learnt the " lay " of the case, can place his fingers in the box required without any effort of memory. It becomes as natural to him as is finding the keys to the expert pianist or typist.

In ordinary typography, the " lay " of the case is fairly standardized, and only slight variations will be found in different printing offices ; but in music printing every office seems to have a different " lay," some following one or other of the suggestions of the typefounders, whilst others have a " lay " of their own originated by the compositors employed. Probably the best way for any firm newly starting in the business of music typesetting is to follow the type-founders' suggestion, unless the compositor has sufficient experience to arrange his own " lay."

CHAPTER XVI

THE ROUTINE OF MUSIC TYPESETTING

IN this chapter we must necessarily use typographic terms which will be unfamiliar to the general reader, and it is not necessary to enter into a lengthy explanation of every expression used. We shall presume, therefore, that we are addressing our remarks to those who are more or less familiar with typography. Others who wish for fuller information are advised to consult such a work as Southward's *Modern Printing*, which fully explains all the technical terms and operations.

The first step for the apprentice to music typesetting is to learn the " lay " of the case ; this will be best done with the typefounders' diagram before him, if the plan of this is to be followed ; but should he be working in a house where the cases are already laid according to some existing plan, it will be better for him to draw a diagram for himself, marking it with the characters he finds in the boxes.

At the same time, he should endeavour, by a study of the synopsis sheet of the typefounder, and with a piece of the printed music before him, to learn the method of setting up the various pieces. He will be aided in this by using a magnifying glass, which may enable him to detect where some of the separate pieces join up.

This is by no means an infallible method, however, as the music printer takes a pride in trying to prevent the joins showing, and many of the apparently simple notes are built up of a number of pieces. For instance, notes are built up of as many as " five sorts " each, and in chords even more.

If the learner has not already a knowledge of the musical notation and the terms employed, the sooner he learns this the more quickly will he progress in the setting of music type. He should, therefore, obtain an elementary book on music, such as *Novello's Primer*, and familiarize himself with the appearance and names of the notes and signs, and their position on the stave. He must also learn how the time is counted, and the value of the notes and rests. Without such knowledge, he would never be able to set up a badly written piece of music " copy " without making numerous mistakes, which would be difficult to correct.

The typefounders' synopsis sheet does not give the names of the characters ; they are identified by numbers, which, while useful enough for ordering up new " sorts," have no significance in the practical work of music typesetting. It is necessary, therefore, for the learner to get to know the names of the pieces and their purpose. The names may vary in different printing offices, and it is only by learning them from the older compositors or by questioning that he will be able to find out.

Having learnt the " lay " of the case and acquired a knowledge of the separate characters, the learner may now proceed to attempt the distribution of a piece of music already set, if he can get the opportunity to do so.

It will be found that the work is made additionally laborious through the electrotyper's wax or the stereotyper's paste or plaster getting into the spaces and making the type stick together. It is desirable that the type should be well cleaned when any such adherent matter is found, or it will upset the regularity of the subsequent setting.

It is necessary to take scrupulous care to return every piece to its right box, and in case of doubt the existing type in the boxes should be examined. The trouble occasioned in subsequent setting through putting " sorts " in the wrong boxes may well be imagined, and an experienced compositor who has to use the cases afterwards would not appreciate the efforts of the beginner.

Assuming that the latter has so far advanced that he may be allowed to proceed with the more important work of setting up a piece of music, it will be best to commence with a simple stave. It is further desirable to choose a piece of printed music, and set it to the same width. In that case, the characters employed can be picked out and the same setting followed.

We give here (Fig. 94) a piece of music set up and stereotyped by Wilson's Printing Co., Ltd., a well-known and old-established London house, which specializes in typographic music printing.

In order that the process of setting up may be better understood, we give a reproduction of a photograph taken to show the piece of music as it lies in the compositor's " stick " partly set. (Fig. 95.)

FIG. 94

EXAMPLE OF MUSIC TYPE SETTING

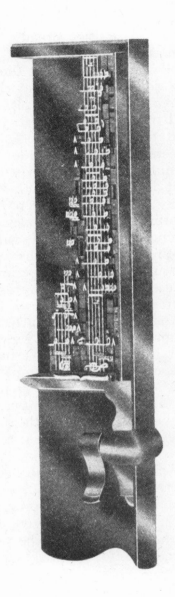

FIG. 95

SHOWING THE APPEARANCE OF MUSIC TYPE WHILE BEING SET UP

So far as the setting up of reprint music is concerned, the work is comparatively easy, especially if the staves are set the same length as in the " copy." If, however, the staves have to be lengthened, some calculation will be required as to whether one or more bars from the next line have to be got in. The stave may have either to be spaced out with rule pieces or compressed if the notes have to be crowded in so as to finish a bar. At the end of the staves, the notes may have to be compressed together ; and, though this is not desirable, it is sometimes unavoidable.

A further consideration is how to secure a suitable position for the turnover at the foot of the page. It is best in this case to pencil out beforehand on the " copy " the divisions for each stave line, and count up the number of ems to be allotted to each bar.

Some compositors first set what is called a " guard line " of quads, with an " em " quad at proper intervals, to show the position of the bars. This guard line is removed when the page is imposed. The more usual way adopted by experienced compositors is to count the number of " ens " to the bar and remember the number.

Another point to recollect is the placing of the minim rest at the end of the last bar. If the piece begins with an imperfect bar, the deficiency must be made up in the last bar.

Whether setting from printed " copy " or from MS., the compositor has to remember that the basis is the " em " body ; and by counting up on the " copy," he knows, when he begins setting, how many bars he will have to the line, how many " ems "

187

to the bar, and how many staves to the page. The system of counting up and pencilling the "copy" as adopted by the engravers (described in Chapter IX) should be followed.

The compositor is expected to know how to give the notes the proper form and position. The MS. is often badly written, and furnishes no guide as to style. In this matter, experience only can guide the compositor, though he may be aided by the study of existing examples of type-printed music.

There is really no convention as to whether stems are turned up or down, nor whether the heads of the notes are turned to the left or right of the stem. Music composers neglect such details, and the compositor must decide for himself which way will look best, at the same time considering how the stave can be most strongly built up. In a sense, he has to build up the staves very much as a bricklayer builds the wall of the house. The bricklayer must lay his bricks so that they will hold together firmly, and in the same way the compositor must place his "stamps" so that they will not readily get displaced and show the joins or produce crooked staves. Thus he finds that it may be best in some parts to turn the stems up and in other parts to turn them down.

We have heard it stated that when the note heads are above the third line, the stems are turned down, and when below the third line the stems are turned up ; also that when notes are on the third line, the stems are turned up if the stem of the following note is up, or down if the next note is down. But really such rules cannot be consistently followed. For instance, it might be quite impossible to follow in chords when there are several heads on one stem.

In two-part music, the stems of the upper part are all up and in the lower part down, whilst in a piece for three voices on one stave the two upper parts are joined together with stems up. The lower voice is apart and has stems down.

The length of the stems varies when hooks and binds are attached. The nominal length of a note is three " ems," viz., for crotchets, one " em " for the head and two " ems " for the stem. For quavers, one " em " for the head, one " em " for the stem, and one " em " for the tail. When binds are used, the stem has to be lengthened as much as may be necessary to reach the bind.

Where two or more notes are bound together, there are certain conventions as to whether the strokes which bind the notes are up, down, or horizontal. If the notes are in a descending scale, the bind descends, and *vice versa*. Notes which are on the same line, or which rise and fall together in a group, should have a horizontal bind. Referring back to the synopsis, it will be seen that there are several kinds of these binds, known as straight, sloping (up and down), and quick or " steep " (up and down). The proper use of all these different kinds must be learnt, but the upward or downward tendency of the notes and the length of the stems will give the clue to the character of the binds required.

A rule for the rise of " slow " and quick or " steep " binds is that when the notes are on adjoining lines or spaces, slow binds are used ; but when on separated

189

lines—" disjunct intervals " in musical language—
the quick or steep binds are used.

In spacing, a black note, whether bound or standing
alone, is reckoned as $1\frac{1}{2}$ " em " in most founts, though
there are a few in which it is only one " em."

Accidentals should be reckoned not as forming
part of the notes, but of the line space. If, therefore, the accidental lies between the bar line and the
next note, one " em " is reckoned ; and if an accidental sharp or flat stands before the note, this sharp
or flat counts as the " em " space. Where there are
several sharps or flats, they are placed close together
without spacing.

Where a dot is placed after a note to lengthen it,
the dot is cast with one piece of the stave line above
it. Dots are also cast with a piece of stave line
above or below ; also two dots under each other,
with their corresponding pieces of stave line. The
bass clef is cast with the dots attached to it.

The signification of the various rests and their
correct position on the stave should be a matter of
careful study. The crotchet and quaver rests are
very similar in appearance, and it is important that
they should not be mistaken. It will be noted that
the former has its curl turned to the right, and the
latter to the left. For greater distinction, it has
become the universal practice to use the new curly
form of crotchet rest. The exact form of the curves
in this sign is varied by different typefounders, but its
general appearance is unmistakable.

The semiquaver rest has two curls, the demisemi-
quaver three, and the semi-demisemiquaver four.

The curls come between the spaces of the stave. These rests are either cast in one piece or in a variety of separate pieces for building up.

All works on the rudiments of music give an illustration of the relative time values of the notes and rests, and a correct knowledge on this point is essential to secure good composing, as the spacing out must be such as to illustrate the time reckoning and enable the music to be easily read.

Correct spacing out is equally as important as the setting of the notes, and certain definite rules must be followed. To get in the necessary number of notes or signs, spaces may have to be taken out. This should be done at the bar lines and at the many syllable words of the text, avoiding places where the words come close to note heads, or stems or ledger lines. In case the last bar or any other bar must be spaced out, this may be done where there is a specially long word in the text, or after a dotted note, or at a bar line, or at the beginning or end of a line.

When several characters read an " en " or more above the stave, the quads and pieces of the stave rule should be set brickwise, so as to prevent the joinings coming under each other, as in this way the stave is strengthened and the joinings do not show badly.

In the case of notes on ledger lines above the stave, these must be set and spaced out with quads before putting in the clef and the bar line.

In setting the words under the staves, a one-" em " space should be left between the words and the lowest line of music above, though this rule is not always followed where the music has to be closely set so as to get as many spaces as possible in a page. Often the words will be set close up to the extremities of the notes or to the first stave line where no notes descend below it.

The words are always placed below the music to which they refer, except in a short score, when they may be placed both above and below the stave for clearness—the words for the treble part above and for the alto part below.

In some cases, it is necessary to make the first stave shorter than the others to allow of the descriptive words " Voice," " Organ," " Violin," etc., to be inserted.

In orchestral scores above the commencement of the stave, directions as to the instruments and voices are set to the words, for instance, " Trumpets," " 1st and 2nd in E," " Second Violin and Tenor." There will also occur such words as " Solo," " Chorus," " Trio," " Duet," etc. These are usually set in small caps. Existing music should be studied for style in these matters. The author's and composer's names are also set, in hymns and songs, immediately above the top stave, the former at the left-hand and the latter at the right-hand side, these names usually being set in small caps.

The words " *with expression*," or the Italian words " *Andante*," " *Molte*," " *Animato*," " *Allegro Moderato*," etc., are set in italics close above the stave to which they refer.

The expressions *cres.* and *dim.* are usually logotypes (cast in one piece), with or without a portion of the stave attached.

192

In the music fount will be found special characters for such signs as

$$f, f\!f, p.$$

These also are cast with and without stave lines attached.

Characters will also be found in the case for all the other signs, such as repetition marks found in music, and their meaning and position should be carefully studied.

In setting up from MS., many abbreviations will be found, and the compositor is expected to understand them and set up the notes in full.

Hymn tunes may be in close or open score. The latter is a score having but one part written on each stave, that is to say there is a stave for each part. In open score, the contralto or alto part is almost always printed in the treble clef. The alto clef (the middle line C) is used in some folio cathedral scores and in some oratorio scores. For the tenor voice, the proper way of indicating the part is by means of the tenor clef (C on the fourth line). The shape of this clef is shown in Fig. 9, Chapter I. The alto clef is the same, but stands on the third line. The line passes between the two curves.

It is said that chorus singers object to learning more than two clefs—treble and bass, so that the general practice is to print the tenor part in the treble clef, and the above clef signs are accordingly seldom seen. In the bass clef, the flats and sharps are placed a line lower.

Southward gives examples of setting various kinds

of music, and the learner would do well to study them. Some of the points we have referred to are there explained more fully.

THE TONIC SOL-FA SYSTEM.

It does not seem necessary to give any extended instructions on the setting of music in the Tonic Sol-fa notation, as it should present no difficulty to any compositor of ordinary intelligence and ability, but he will do the work more easily if he has a knowledge of the system so as to know how to translate it.

The notes are cast to " ems " or even division of " ems," so that it is easy to reckon the spacing.

Messrs. J. Curwen & Sons, Ltd., have brought the printing of this kind of music to great perfection, and the writer has had the privilege of visiting their extensive works and having the methods explained. In preparing " copy " for the Tonic Sol-fa, a squared paper is used, each square representing a pulse or beat. The basis of the type being the " em " body, the notes can be easily counted up on the copy, so that the compositor knows how many bars go to the line and how many staves to the page.

Frequently the Tonic Sol-fa notation is set under the music of the old notation, and Messrs. Curwen do a large amount of music typesetting in that way.

The sizes are, in printers' terms, Minion, Bourgeois, Pica, and Small Pica, together with an old English " black " cut specially for the firm. Most of the typefounders now supply founts for Tonic Sol-fa, and

194

special type for the blind is also used. The Tonic Sol-fa is also punched on engraved plates.

On the " em " body basis, a " middle space " (in printers' measure) is used for dot, comma, inverted comma, and octave marks ; accents are on an " en " body, as are the rules. The letter **m** is contracted to an " en " body, which makes it look attenuated, like the **m** stamped by a typewriter, but it makes the spacing easier to have it so.

It may be added that the type for Tonic Sol-fa is cast on the point system, which makes justification easy.

The price of type for Tonic Sol-fa is much less than that for the old notation and, as there are fewer characters, it comes much cheaper to install the founts. According to Shanks's latest price list, Long Primer is 7s. 6d. ; Bourgeois, 8s. ; Brevier, 8s. 5d. ; and Nonpareil, 11s.

GREGORIAN, PLAIN-SONG, OR CHANT MUSIC.

The terms Plain-song, Plaint Chant, Chant, and Gregorian are identical for indicating the special kind of music traditionally used in the Western Church.

In ancient times, plain-song was often called " Prick Song," from the dots or points being pricked on the stave by a sharp point. The " pricking of musick bookes " was a term employed in the olden times to express the writing of music.

This kind of music is seldom met with in the ordinary course of commercial music printing, but most music printers have a fount or two of the

195

Hands Across the Sea.

10 Point.

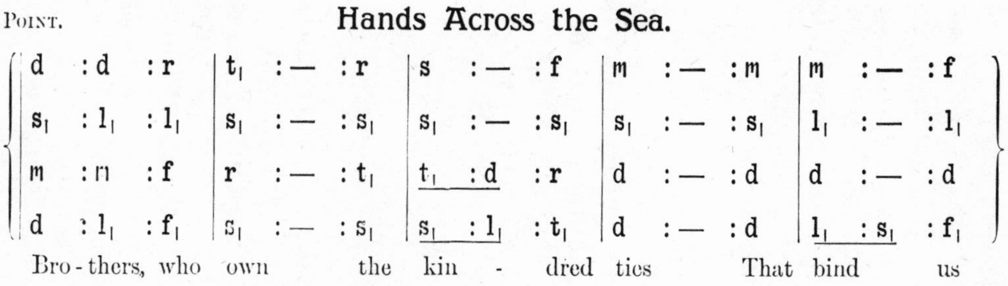

d	:d	:r	t₁	:—	:r	s	:—	:f	m	:—	:m	m	:—	:f
s₁	:l₁	:l₁	s₁	:—	:s₁	s₁	:—	:s₁	s₁	:—	:s₁	l₁	:—	:l₁
m	:n	:f	r	:—	:t₁	t₁	:d	:r	d	:—	:d	d	:—	:d
d	:l₁	:f₁	s₁	:—	:s₁	s₁	:l₁	:t₁	d	:—	:d	l₁	:s₁	:f₁

Bro-thers, who own the kin - dred ties That bind us

FIG. 96

SPECIMEN OF 10 POINT TONIC SOL-FA MUSIC, BY MILLER AND RICHARD

Gregorian type and will set up works with it if called upon to do so. Our work would not be complete without a reference to it.

In some Hymnals, both plain-song and ordinary notation are given in the accompanying music of certain hymns.

Most music engravers have sets of punches for engraving plain-song, and the typefounders supply the type for it in one or more sizes. About fifty characters are employed in setting this kind of music, when the stave lines are printed in black at the same time as the notes, and ten characters only when the stave lines are printed in red at a separate operation.

Messrs. R. H. Stevens & Co. cast their chant music on a Ruby body ; but Messrs. Shanks have three sizes, viz., Nonpareil (6 point), Brevier (8 point), and English (14 point). We give the point equivalents, although, as previously stated, the point system is not used for music type. The two smaller sizes are for single printing (i.e. notes and staves together).

The last-mentioned firm have cut punches from MS. music supplied by the Vatican authorities, having made the type to a special order for the printers to the cathedrals of Tournai and Malines. The firm still have the punches and matrices in their possession, but do not supply the type from them unless permission is obtained from the Vatican. This has only once been granted in the case of a small fount supplied by Oxford University.

H. Dessain, of Malines, was a famous printer of Gregorian music before the war, but during the war he was a refugee in London, his splendid founts of

197

music type having been destroyed during the German invasion.

Deberny, of Paris, is a well-known maker of music type, and supplies a 5-point body. This, however, would not be available for English printers owing to the height of French type being different to ours.

A good example of Gregorian music printing, with red staves, bearing the imprint of Masters, Aldersgate Street, E.C., is to be seen in the Blades' Library.

The music for plain-song is written on four-line staves, these lines being often printed red in ancient music, but now more generally in black. In this case the staves are built up with the notes, as in the modern notation when typographically printed.

The four lines with the spaces below, between, and above them serve to place the nine different diatonic sounds. Most melodies in plain-song are of moderate extent from the lowest to the highest sounds ; hence four lines with their spaces serve the purpose.

The Rev. Thomas Helmore, in his book *Plain-Song* (Novello Primers), says—

There is no essential difference between the characters of the old notation and those answering to them in that more modern ; and a person who really understands the one, can easily learn to decipher the other. There is no more real difference between the Old English black letter print and common print, the former in ancient and the latter in modern books.

The Gregorian notation consists of three distinct shapes of notes, viz.—

FIG. 97

LONG   BREVE   SEMIBREVE

The clefs are placed on the line most convenient for

the compass of the melody, which usually does not exceed an octave. The principal clefs are shown on the next page (Fig. 98). They give their own name to the particular line they stand on, that is to say the line passing through the two thick slanting strokes of each, as shown. The other lines take their names accordingly. This is a point which should be remembered by the compositor learning the system.

The scale of the Gregorian notation has already been shown in Fig. 5, Chapter I.

In modern type, the notes are usually square, but in the old music they were often oblong. The shapes of the notes were brought about by the method of writing the manuscript music. The stem or tail of the " long " is a relic of the ancient notation, in which the note was marked by an upward stroke, whilst the lozenge form of the semibreve is due to the pen being held in a slanting position when writing the descending notes. This latter supposition is borne out by the fact that in well-written old manuscript music this lozenge or diamond form only occurs in the descending passages. Manuscript music also exists in which square notes are replaced with the diamond shape, while in others, every single note has a stem or tail.

The shape of the notes does not, as in the case of the old notation, express differences of time value.

Single and double bar lines are used as in the modern notation, and brackets are employed when required.

A vertical line is used in the old Gregorian MSS.,

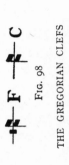

F_{IG.} 98

THE GREGORIAN CLEFS

RUBY CHANT MUSIC.

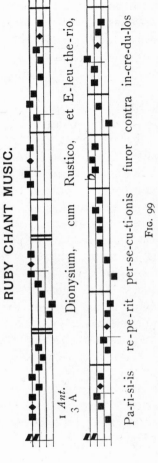

F_{IG.} 99

SPECIMEN OF CHANT MUSIC TYPE, BY R. H. STEVENS AND CO.

and in some printed books such lines are used to divide the notes of one word from those of another, but this must not be confused with the modern bar. A double line marks the end of a sentence.

No accidentals are used with the exception that B may be changed to

$$B\flat$$

The sign will accordingly be found in plain-song music, and stands in a space, as will be seen in the specimen of Chant Music. (Fig. 99.)

In attempting to decipher ancient plain-song music, it will be found somewhat puzzling, owing to some different signs being used. This is fully explained in Helmore's book.

It does not seem necessary to give any special directions for setting Gregorian music type, as the principles are the same as for the modern notation and the work is much simpler.

We give an example of this kind of music from the specimen book of Messrs. R. H. Stevens & Co. This shows the simple forms of type characters employed.

CHAPTER XVII

STEREOTYPING AND ELECTROTYPING MUSIC

TYPE-SET pages of music are invariably stereotyped or electrotyped instead of being printed direct. This has the double advantage of enabling the type to be distributed and used again for setting up further pages, whilst the plates can be kept after printing for the production of further editions. Without the aid of stereotyping, a much larger amount of type would be required and, as music type is expensive, this is a serious matter. The process of stereotyping has, therefore, come to be recognized and adopted as a valuable auxiliary to typographic music printing. Without it there would not have been the same progress in this kind of music printing. As it is, stereotyping has enabled works to be produced at a much cheaper rate than would otherwise have been the case.

The process of stereotyping was invented by William Ged, a goldsmith, of Edinburgh, so far back as the year 1725, and, curiously enough, the method he devised for making the mould in plaster is the one found best for stereotyping music to-day, although the process is not now worked in the same way. The old method consisted in pouring a thick layer of plaster direct on to the type forme, and leaving it to set and dry. This was a troublesome process, as the forme had first to be " floated " (i.e. a thin layer of plaster was poured over the forme so as to fill up the deep spaces, which otherwise might have made it difficult to remove the plaster cast). The " floating " had to be dry before it was possible to put on the thick layer for the mould. As the latter would be from $\frac{1}{2}$ in. to $\frac{3}{4}$ in. thick, it took a long time to dry, and there was a risk of breakage in getting it off. Moreover, it was necessary to use a special casting-box for pouring the molten metal on to the mould. In every way, the old process was very tedious, whilst the method now adopted is extremely simple and speedy.

The procedure is as follows—

A sheet of tough paper is thoroughly wetted and laid on a smooth stone. Two lengths of printer's brass rule (four-to-pica thickness) are then laid on the paper, one on each side. These rules serve to determine the thickness of the coating as the plaster is poured between and levelled by drawing over it, in scraper fashion, a piece of brass rule, the ends of which rest on the two side rules. The thickness of coating thus obtained will be about $\frac{1}{24}$ in. The plaster is allowed to partly set and the side rules are then removed. The paper with its adhering coating of plaster is then lifted from the stone and laid face down on the type forme, which has been brushed over with an oily brush. The forme bearing the plaster-paper, covered with a piece of blanket, is then pushed under a powerful screw or toggle press, and is given a good squeeze. Then the forme is placed on a shelf over which is a series of gas tubes, with an iron plate above to deflect the heat downward on to the back of the mould. In about half an hour the mould is dry, and by tapping the back of the forme with a small wooden mallet, the mould springs away from the type, and is lifted off crisp and dry as a biscuit. The mould is then placed in the stereotyper's casting-box and the metal poured in as usual.

Only one cast can be taken from a plaster mould as a rule, as the surface is generally broken or cracked in pulling it away from the cast. If duplicates are required, it is necessary to take more moulds.

One advantage of this plaster method is that the stave lines can be ruled on the mould so as to remedy any imperfect joining up of the lines formed by the separate pieces of type. These bad joins show in the mould as slight projections above the level of the lines, and by drawing the sharp edge of a piece of printer's rule along the lines, the projections are removed, leaving the lines continuous. If carefully done, this ruling greatly improves the appearance of the print taken from the stereo. Fig. 100 should be compared with Fig. 94.

There is another process of stereotyping, which is almost universally used for making newspaper and book plates, known as the papier mâché or " flong " process. This method may sometimes be adopted for music formes, but it is not a desirable one, as it subjects the type to a good deal of wear and tear. Music type is much more liable to injury than ordinary type, and is also much more expensive to replace, so that it is decidedly disadvantageous to use the papier mâché process for this work. This will be better appreciated if we describe the process, so that the two methods may be compared.

It is appropriate to say here that, whichever process is used, the type forme must be prepared for stereotyping by surrounding the page with clumps of metal, forming a sort of frame about $\frac{1}{2}$ in. in width. These clumps are the same height as the type, and act as bearers to prevent any damage to the edges of the type page, also avoiding the moulding material being cut through or impressed too deeply at the edges. The impression of the clumps also forms a margin for the gauges of the casting-box to rest on, so that they may be laid in their proper position and be retained there. The page with its clumps is locked up in a " chase " (i.e. an iron frame which secures the type from falling apart). The type surface is well cleaned to free it from ink and dirt, and is brushed over with an oily brush, so as to prevent the mould from sticking.

The papier mâché used for moulding is called the " flong," a corruption of the French word *flan*, so named from the resemblance of the material to the thin dough rolled out by the pastry cook to make a *flan*. The " flong " consists of layers of tissue and blotting paper on a brown paper backing, each sheet being thickly coated with a special paste. There may be one layer of brown paper, one of blotting, and three of tissue to make a good " flong." Sometimes the surface is faced with a creamy composition, which sets like a hard enamel. The " flong " is kept in a damp, flabby condition, and is laid with the

Fig. 100

SPECIMEN OF MUSIC TYPE SETTING SHOWING IMPERFECT JOINING OF
THE RULES, WHICH IS CORRECTED BY RULING ON THE MATRIX

tissue paper face down on the type forme. It is then beaten with a flat, stiff brush with long handle, so as to force the soft " flong " into the hollows of the type. A skilful stereotyper can perform this operation of beating very uniformly. When the beating is done, the forme bearing the matrix is placed under a screw press, which has a bed heated by steam or gas, and it is left there until the " flong " is baked quite dry. This only takes a few minutes. When the mould is stripped off, it will be found a perfect matrix of the type, and is then called the matrix.

This matrix is laid in the casting-box, which consists of a heavy iron bed and platen, closing and opening like a book. The matrix is held in its place by strips of steel or brass, called gauges, surrounding three sides, the top being left open for pouring in the metal. These gauges regulate the thickness by holding the matrix a distance from the front plate or platen of the box when it is closed. The thickness of the plate is usually a " pica " in printer's measure, and equals $\frac{1}{6}$ in. In some cases plates are cast "long primer " thickness, which is slightly less. These thin plates are for mounting on iron beds on the printing machines ; but when the plates are mounted on wood, they are usually " pica " thickness. Casts may also be made full type height, but this is not often done owing to the great weight of metal required and the consequent expense. To remedy this and still have the advantage of casting to type height, special cores may be used in the casting-box to give a kind of arching to the back of the cast.

The stereotype metal consists of an alloy of lead,

tin, and antimony, which is melted and poured into the casting-box, where it runs into every hollow of the matrix and forms an exact replica of the original type page. When cool, the plate is removed, trimmed, and nailed to the wood block, either mahogany or oak being used.

The casts are sometimes planed on the back by a special machine. This is done when the plates are for mounting on iron beds, as it is necessary they should all be exactly the same height, but for mounting on wood the backs are generally left as they come from the casting-box.

The stereotype plates thus obtained, either from the plaster or papier mâché moulds, can then be printed from exactly in the same way as if the original type forme was used. The result is never so good as that from the original type, but it is considered good enough for cheap editions. If the plates are nickel plated, as is sometimes done, they will print better and wear longer.

One advantage of the papier mâché process is that several plates can be cast, as a rule, from the same matrix, so that duplicates can be made for printing future editions, or for running additional machines in case a large edition is to be printed. Sometimes the matrices are preserved for future use.

ELECTROTYPING.

The process of electrotyping, though yielding better results than stereotyping, is the more costly of the two methods, the price being at least double that for stereos. It also presents some difficulties, chief

208

amongst which is the fact that the wax used for moulding clings to the deep interstices between the notes and staves. To overcome this, the forme is usually " floated " with plaster of Paris, as described in an earlier part of this chapter in dealing with the plaster stereotyping process. This floating makes the spaces shallower, whilst leaving a sufficient relief to the type characters to enable them to be moulded. Music printers do not like this " floating " with plaster, because it is difficult to remove when the type is distributed. This is probably one of the reasons why electrotyping is in disfavour.

When the forme is thus prepared, the next step is to pour a layer of melted beeswax (to which sometimes plumbago and other ingredients are added) on to a metal plate as large as the forme to be moulded. The surface of the beeswax is brushed over with finely-powdered blacklead, as is also the forme. This prevents adherence of the wax and makes the surface of the mould electrically conductive. The wax plate, or " case " as it is called, is laid face down on the forme and pressure is applied by means of a powerful hydraulic press. The resulting mould, which reproduces the type even more perfectly than the plaster or papier mâché " flong," is trimmed free from the surplus wax, which has been squeezed out at the edges, and then polished with blacklead. It is then suspended in a solution of copper sulphate, on a brass or copper rod connected to the conductors of the current from the dynamo, a copper plate being placed opposite and close to the moulded surface. The action of the current causes copper to be deposited on the surface until a sufficient thickness is obtained to allow the copper " shell," as it is called, to be stripped off. This shell is coated on the back with melted tinfoil, to act as a solder ; and is then " backed-up " by pouring soft type metal in a molten state on to it to the thickness required, this being determined by the gauges surrounding the shell. After cooling, the plate is trimmed off at the margins and planed on the back to the required thickness of $\frac{1}{6}$ in. It is then nailed to a wood mount to bring it to type height, when it is ready for printing.

The electrotype or stereotype plates can, of course, be kept in the same way as pewter plates for printing future editions, with the difference that they are ready for printing without further treatment. The pewter plates require to have transfers pulled from them and put down on to zinc plates, unless the latter have been preserved after printing the previous edition.

Although the first cost of the typographic printing, supplemented by stereotyping or electrotyping, is several times greater than by the lithographic method, it is the cheapest in the end where large editions are anticipated.

On the relative cost of engraved and typographically-printed music, it is interesting to quote the following from Novello's *Short History of Cheap Music*—

The probable number of copies to be sold must decide whether it is advisable to produce the work on engraved plates or by movable music type. The cost of producing a page of music on a pewter plate is comparatively small, and there is the further advantage of being able to print fifty copies from it as conveniently as any number of hundreds, thereby saving the accumulation of useless stock and loss of interest on cost of paper—great disadvantages in a work of slow or doubtful sale or the demand for which is likely to be limited. The disadvantage of this mode is the early wearing out of the plates (from 1,300 to 2,000 impressions), according to the goodness of the workmanship ; also the comparatively high cost of printing. One page produced by music types must be costly because types are expensive to purchase and require considerable skill to compose them into the required page ; but for any work of which a large number of impressions is wanted, they offer many advantages. By the process of stereo, a very large number of pages can be successively produced from a fount of type, and still leave the type at perfect liberty to compose fresh pages. Movable music type is particularly well adapted for the production of books on the science of music, or where musical examples are subordinate to the descriptions or comments which form the main part of the work. Of the disadvantages of music type, an important one has been removed by the increased varieties of characters ; and any music, however complicated, can now be produced with these. To sum up, for hundreds, plates are best ; for thousands, type is preferable.

Mr. Novello gives an example of the respective cost of typographic music compared with plate-printed music, and, though the prices would not apply at the present day, the relative proportions would be similar. For an edition of 200 copies produced in the old way from engraved plates (he says) the cost would be £35 10s. ; whilst, from type, an edition of 2,000 copies would be produced for £170 10s. In the one case, the cost divided among 200 purchasers was about 3s. 6d. per copy, whilst it was only 1s. 9d. per copy when divided among 2,000 purchasers. Had it not been for typographic printing, it is hardly likely that so many as 20,000 copies of " The Messiah " and similar large numbers of other works would have been sold, as was the case at the date of the publication of this pamphlet.

When Mr. Novello speaks of the wear of the engraved plates, he is considering direct printing from the plates ; but where lithography is employed, this disadvantage does not occur, as only transfers are taken from the plates.

The advantage referred to of being able to print music-type with text also applies to printing it in illustrated books and magazines.

Probably one reason why typographical music has fallen into disrepute is through publishers making the mistake of crowding it into small pages and printing it on poor paper. Engraved music is much easier to read ; it is better spaced, and there are no breaks in the lines and notes as is so often the case with type-set music. It has been well said that a page of engraved music can be made " to look like a picture," but no one would say that of a page of type-set music.

CHAPTER XVIII

FROM time to time, as we show in the next chapter, there have been attempts to supersede the method of engraving music on pewter plates ; but these methods have, for the most part, been unsuccessful, and the old method holds its own, in spite of some disadvantages. Its most serious rival has been the autographic process.

THE AUTOGRAPHIC PROCESS.

This method, sometimes called the auto-lithographic process, consists in drawing the music on lithographic transfer paper. The name implies that the composer's own writing is reproduced, but few composers would find themselves able to write on lithographic transfer paper with the greasy ink which has to be used to facilitate transfer. It is possible to dispense with the transfer paper (which has a starchy or glutinous surface) and use a glazed writing paper, but the greasy ink must still be used, and it is apt to produce thick writing unless skilfully used with fine pens. Autographic music is, therefore, more usually re-drawn by experienced lithographic draughtsmen.

The disadvantages of the method are summed up as follows—

1. The time required for executing good work by

auto-lithography (i.e. the production of the transfer) is longer than for engraving, and this makes the work of preparation more expensive.

2. The impossibility of inserting the words on the music at the same time as the staves involves the employment of a typographic process in conjunction with the transfer drawing. The words are usually set up in type ; a transfer print made from the same ; and, after being cut into suitable strips, pasted on to the transfer drawing in the proper place.

3. The finished transfer may be absolutely spoilt in transferring, and in such case would have to be drawn again.

4. As nothing remains of the original work after transferring, the drawing will have to be done again for a new edition, unless the work is kept on the stones or plates. To do this is costly, more so, in fact, than preserving the pewter plates, which in themselves have an intrinsic value if at any time they have to be discarded.

However, it will be useful to describe this auto-lithographic process in case any of our readers should see some useful application of it. One advantage is that it may be employed where a music engraver is not available.

Henri Robert says the transfer drawing is done on a paper which has received one or two coatings of fish glue. We should think that there is no necessity for preparing a special paper of this kind, as numerous excellent ready-made papers are on the market. The paper should have faint lines in squares of 2 mms. to serve as a guide for drawing the staves and placing the notes. Such squared transfer paper can be bought ready-prepared equally as well as plain transfer paper.

It is necessary to take great care not to soil the surface of the paper by marking it with greasy fingers, or in any other way. To prevent this, a hand-rest

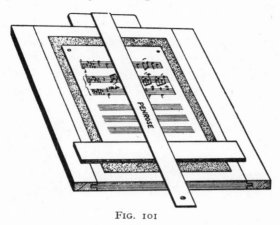

FIG. 101

DRAWING BOARD FOR TRANSFER WRITING

is used in conjunction with a special drawing board, as shown in Fig. 101.

A sheet of autographic paper is squarely fixed on the board, with a piece of thick blotting paper of the same size underneath. A frame of thick cardboard rests on the transfer paper and surrounds it. On this frame, a strip of wood rests and forms a support for the hand.

The work is drawn the right way, not reversed as in engraving. This is obvious when it is remembered that the transferring to the stone turns it the reversed way, and when the print is taken from the stone it comes the right way again.

The manuscript is first marked off as for engraving, so as to make the music fit the pages to be printed.

For rapidly obtaining the spacing of the lines of the stave, a small punch with five points is used, these points being spaced according to the size of the staves in the music to be produced. Having impressed the points on the paper, the lines of the stave are drawn singly with a drawing pen. Special pens with five nibs in one holder have been made for ruling the scores in manuscript music, but so far as we know have not been used for transfer drawing. They would probably scratch up the surface of the transfer paper and rule unequally.

The staves can be ruled with a small roller with raised lines on it. This roller is inked with lithographic transfer ink, and it is then pressed on to the paper, guided by a straight edge. If properly used, this is a much more rapid way of ruling the staves than drawing them singly with the pen. There are several patterns of this instrument, and one has a self-inking arrangement. The rollers can be changed in the holder as required for different sizes of staves. Being of French manufacture, the spacing is in millimetres, and there are ten sizes. The following are the three first numbers, with their English equivalents—

No. 1. Height of stave $8\frac{1}{2}$ mm. (about $\frac{3}{8}$ in.)
,, 2. ,, ,, 8 ,, (,, $\frac{5}{16}$ in.)
,, 3. ,, ,, $7\frac{1}{2}$,, (,, $\frac{9}{32}$ in.)

The height of the stave is, of course, the distance between the first and fifth lines.

The notes and signs can be drawn with a pen or a line brush ; but to secure uniformity, it is better to stamp them with steel punches, which are cut in

FIG. 102

TYPEHOLDER FOR STAMPING

reverse, so as to give a print the right way on the paper.

Instead of steel punches, it would be possible to use music type, as this already has the characters reversed ; but a suitable holder would be required to hold the type, such as the bookbinder's typeholder, or a little instrument which is used for stamping names of places on maps. (Fig. 102.) With such

217

a holder as the last mentioned, it would be possible to print in the words.

The punch or type is lightly inked by means of a printer's composition roller. Anyone not familiar with handling a roller and ink may probably make the mistake of applying too much ink, so that when the impression is made the print would have a squashed effect. To avoid this, the ink should be used as stiff as possible, and it should be well distributed by running the roller to and fro on a slab, so as to get a very thin and uniform coating.

The drawing of the stems of the notes and the bars is done last, using a square and a ruling pen charged with auto-litho transfer ink.

Corrections are made by means of a small camel hair brush dipped in benzole. This is passed over the sign to be corrected until the ink is removed ; then the place where the benzole has been applied is allowed to dry before drawing or impressing a new sign.

The transfer sheets, when finished, are kept flat and are separated from one another by sheets of thin white paper. They must not be pressed, and should be delivered at once to the printer, so that the ink will be as fresh as possible.

Two kinds of ink are used for autographic transfers. One is a greasy paste-like ink, called " Type-transfer Ink," which is used for inking the type or punches, and it is distributed with the roller on a stone inking slab. The other is lithographic writing ink, sometimes called " Tusche." This ink is sold in flat sticks wrapped in tinfoil, somewhat like tablets of chocolate in outward appearance. The principal makers are

218

Lemercier and Vanhymbeck, both of whom are located in France.

The ink is prepared for use as follows : A shallow saucer is slightly heated over a gas flame or other source of heat and, when sufficiently warm to soften the ink, the stick, with the tinfoil removed from one end, is rubbed against the bottom of the vessel, which is thus soon covered with a black sticky mass. A few drops of distilled or rain water are added, and are mixed with the ink by rubbing with the end of the stick of ink or with the ball of a finger until sufficient fluidity is obtained to enable the ink to flow from the pen. This is ascertained by frequent trials. The reason for using distilled or rain water is that the lime in ordinary tap water curdles the soap in the ink and prevents a free flowing solution being obtained. It is necessary to make up the ink every day, as it rapidly deteriorates. A cardboard cover, with a small hole in it for dipping through, should be provided, in order to prevent dust or other foreign matter getting into it.

Those who do not care for the trouble of preparing ink in this way, as they may only require to use it very occasionally and to a limited extent, can purchase a ready-prepared ink called " Liquid Auto-litho Ink " or " Autographic Ink." Some kinds of this ink have a yellowish appearance, and it is then not so easy to see whether the lines are well covered as when using ink freshly rubbed up ; but it saves a good deal of trouble and, as a rule, its use offers no difficulty in making the transfer. This ink is often used on a hard glazed writing paper, when preparing architects' specifications with it ; and it would be worth trying whether a similar paper could be used for music writing, as the transfer paper is by no means easy to work on when first essayed by the inexperienced.

It may be added that special pens have been made suitable for drawing the black and white notes, and also other pens for the ties, slurs, etc.

This method of writing the music can also be applied to the preparation of copies for photo-process reproduction. In this case, thin Bristol board or a stiff, smooth, white drawing paper should be used. The best ink is the waterproof Indian ink for the pen or brush. The notes can either be stamped or drawn. In the former case, a good black printing ink, used very stiff, should be employed, applying the ink with a composition roller. The words can be printed on separate sheets, cut up, and pasted on the drawings in the proper position, so that the whole is reproduced together.

A skilled lithographic draughtsman can draw the music direct on a lithographic stone or upon a zinc plate, but this method is hardly ever resorted to, as it would be as tedious as punching, and more expensive.

It has been suggested that in the case of standard music books of large circulation, it would be preferable to punch and engrave the music by hand and to make zinco blocks from the proofs or transfers, so as to print by the ordinary letterpress method than to set up the music in type. This plan would be more satisfactory and equally as cheap as the ordinary method of litho printing.

CHAPTER XIX

VARIOUS SUGGESTED IMPROVEMENTS IN MUSIC PRINTING

NOTWITHSTANDING the improvements made in casting music type, its setting remains to this day a tedious and expensive matter, and hardly less so is the process of engraving the plates. Naturally this has led to numerous attempts being made by inventors to devise new processes for superseding the old ones. It is a singular fact, however, that not one of these new methods has, so far as we know, come into practical use.

Some of these inventions sought to change the notation by reducing the number of characters, or altering the arrangement of the stave. Others attempted to reduce the number of type characters by printing the stave and notes separately. A further group of inventors attacked the problem of engraving the plates, and sought mechanical means to simplify it. Still another group attempted to do away both with the typesetting and the engraving by adapting the principle of the typewriting machine for the purpose of either stamping the notes into some soft material to form a matrix for stereotyping and electrotyping ; or by stamping on to transfer paper to form a lithographic transfer ; or printing on to ordinary white paper to form a copy for photo-lithography or photo-zincography. Finally, there was the class who endeavoured to dispense with the writing, printing, or stamping by having a set of characters which could be arranged and photographed.

It is astonishing to find what an immense amount of misplaced ingenuity has been displayed in such inventions, as they do not appear to have received any encouragement from the trade they were designed to assist.

We propose to summarize such of these inventions as we have been able to find records of in the Patent Office and elsewhere. We do this not because of any hope that the ideas may be revived and put to use, but as a matter of interest to those who wish to know all about music engraving and printing, and also perhaps to warn off the would-be inventor from following on paths which have already been well trodden, and have unfortunately led to nowhere.

We have not attempted to record these inventions in chronological order, but rather to classify them into groups, showing how one inventor's work has overlapped that of another. We have already referred to several of the early inventions in music engraving and printing in previous chapters, and the ensuing record refers therefore to comparatively recent efforts.

In the Blades' Library there is a report in French on a method of printing music from movable type invented by M. Duguet in 1833, and for which a medal was awarded by the Athenée des Arts. No details are given, but the claim is made that 3,000 copies of a piece of four pages can be produced in a

222

day at a price of 20 centimes, instead of 1·50 fr., by the ordinary process.

Another report to be found in the same library is on a new process of typographic music by M. Duverger, submitted to the Society of Agriculture, etc., at Douai in 1835. This inventor claims to have remedied all previous drawbacks to the typographic method, but does not divulge the secret of his process. He says the staves at first glance appear continuous, and a single pull suffices for the printing. The composition is said to cost twice the price of engraving, but that the economy in printing and on the paper compensates for this.

The trouble of getting the separate elements of the staves into alignment and to appear continuous was always one of the difficulties in the early typographic music, and this, together with the difficulty of setting up and justifying so many little pieces of type, led to the invention of various processes for music printing. Some system of double printing was the basis of several of these processes, but it is said that owing to the necessity of damping the paper it was difficult to get register. Paper is now usually printed dry, so that this trouble would not now be met with.

One ingenious way was to arrange brass characters on a block of wood, and cement them down with plaster. The tympan of the press was made to turn on an axis after taking the impression from the notes, receiving next the impression of the staves without removing the sheet.

Messrs. Clowes preserve as a curiosity in their printing works the interesting results of an ingenious though unsuccessful attempt to supersede the setting up of type for music printing. These are a couple of blocks, the exact history of which has been forgotten, showing that the various notes, consisting of pieces of copper, have been driven into a block of soft wood, whilst the words are in ordinary type let into a space pierced through the block. In one of these blocks the lines of the stave are also driven in, but in the other there are no stave lines ; and it was evidently intended to print the staves by a separate impression. It is not surprising that such a process never came into practical use, for the production of the blocks must have been even more tedious than setting type.

There is a record of Edward Cowper patenting in 1827 a process of setting up the notes in copper type, and printing them and the staves at separate operations. The results were said to be excellent, and several printers used the process, but it is added that they eventually reverted to engraving.

H. A. L. Chaix and M. C. A. Bourgeaux (Patent No. 6404, 1911) proposed to print by the typographic method from two or more formes used successively, one for the stave lines, bars, phrasing marks, libretto, and all signs printed outside the staves, together with all signs that could not form part of the first forme. The heads of the notes are in one forme and the tails (with or without hooks) are printed by another forme.

A. Chassefoin (No. 16802, 1886) proposed to set up the notes in type, the characters being split up into parts, so that the sections come between the stave lines, which are very thin continuous brass rules.

When locked up, the parts come together and appear continuous.

No. 17121 (1897) is by the same inventor. The space blanks separating the thin rules are hollowed or shaped at their ends, so as to give support to the rules.

A patent by L. Normandy (No. 2307, of 1855) describes a method by which the lines of the musical scale are printed in black and two other colours. Three interlocked plates in relief are employed. They are separately inked and, when fitted together for printing, are suitably clamped with their printing surfaces in the same plane. A later patent (No. 868, of 1856) of the same inventor explains that the first line is printed in green, the second in black, the third is dotted in red, the fourth black, and the fifth red. Each colour corresponds to a particular note, so that the position of, say, the green line in the scale indicates the key in which the particular composition is written. A platen press with three plates is (says the inventor) preferably used in printing music in this manner.

Gustav Scheurmann invented, in 1856, a system of printing music from movable type at two impressions. His patents are numbered 1170 and 2390, of 1856, and the specification says that the notes and spaces are separate pieces ; but tie lines for the notes are continuous, and are cast on stepped bodies, so that the pieces of the notes may be fitted to them. The slurs are printed from separate type characters. Two formes are made up, one with the staves and the other with the notes, and the two are locked up together in a double chase. The platen of the press is the size of one forme, first one and then the other being pushed under the platen. The tympan which carries the paper is so arranged that it can be laid down first on one forme to receive the impression of the staves, and then on the other to receive the notes, the register of the two being maintained by the accuracy of the mechanism. The two impressions may be in different colours. It is mentioned in the patent that a stereotype may be used for the notes and rules for the staves. Scheurmann's method is described in the *Society of Arts Journal* (Vol. VI, 1858, p. 458).

Even so late as 1884, this method of double printing attracted the inventor ; and Jabez Francis, of Rochford, brought out what he called " Universal Music Type." The staves were printed from a forme made up of brass rules, the notes being impressed from a second forme. Two chases with registering devices were used, so as to get the notes in the correct position. It was claimed that a smaller fount of type sufficed, whilst the pieces were more easily set up, each note being cast on one body. Besides, the music might be printed in a variety of keys by shifting the page of notes up or down, and changing the signatures and accidents.

Of late years, inventors have turned their attention to mechanical devices on the principle of the typewriter or typesetting machines for producing music.

One of the earliest inventors in this field was Sig. Angelo Tessaro, of Padua, and it was stated in 1888 that he had perfected his tachygraphic machine by which the cost of music printing would be enormously reduced. He intended to apply his system to typography in substitution for the ordinary movable types. It was further stated that the machine had been bought by Messrs. Home & Son, Edinburgh, in association with Messrs. Novello and several other London publishers ; and also by the firm of Röder, of Leipzig.

This method, which was first employed in the well-known music-printing house of Ricordi, in Milan, consisted in the employment of a machine which stamped the notes into a zinc plate, which was supported on a travelling table.

The system was eventually found to be unpractical, and it is not now used so far as we can ascertain. The principal drawback to it was the difficulty of making corrections.

We are informed that Messrs. Novello long ago ceased to have any interest in the invention, whilst Messrs. Home & Son are no longer to be found in business in Edinburgh. Messrs. Röder apparently did not find it necessary to dispense with their large staff of engravers on account of it.

F. Dogilbert, of Brussels, has constructed a machine which was evidently on similar lines as that of Tessaro, and reference to this is made in a later part of this chapter.

At the time of writing, we hear that Dr. Reginald S. Clay, London, has made a machine for punching the notes on music plates, the idea being to merely punch the note heads, signs, etc., and finish the rest of the plate by hand. An important feature of the machine is an almost automatic method of spacing out the notes. We have seen a model of the proposed machine in operation, and it seems decidedly promising.

One of Signor Tessaro's patents (No. 16547, 1887) describes an apparatus for writing music to be transferred to stone or zinc for printing. A zinc plate carries a sheet of transfer paper, which is mounted on a turntable, and provided with a traversing screw so as to move up and down the base board. A frame carries a sort of square, the arms forming which can be moved along longitudinally and transversely, and may be locked. The frame is graduated. To the squares a stave-ruling device can be clamped (this is an ivory roller with ridges on it). There is a note-printing device, the characters being either separate or mounted on a wheel. A ruling pen is provided, and there are devices for ruling curved lines.

C. A. Ker, of Glasgow, between 1889 and 1891, took out three patents for mechanical methods of producing music printing plates. No. 9407 of 1889 describes how the music to be copied is first traced to a large scale on a sheet of metal or cardboard, which is held down on a table so that the tracer point of a pantograph can be passed over it, the reducing arm carrying a point which engraves the notes on a copper printing cylinder. The outlines only of the heads of the crotchets, quavers, and other solid-headed notes are traced, and the central portion which is to print black is deepened by etching with acid.

In two subsequent patents, No. 6835 and No. 14057, both of 1891, the same inventor describes an apparatus

228

for punching metal or cardboard sheets, means being also provided for drawing the stave lines. To enable zinc plates to be employed, a heating device is used, apparently for softening the metal.

W. A. Ker, brother of the above inventor, in Patent No. 2681 of 1892 describes another method, using a pantograph to guide a spring punch, which is pressed by the hand, for stamping the notes on lead, cardboard, or other material coated with wax. After the punching is completed, the wax surface is dusted over with blacklead, and copper is deposited upon it. The copper shell is afterwards backed up with soft type metal in the usual manner employed for the production of electrotypes.

W. H. Lock and J. Broadhouse, in Patent No. 482 of 1900, describe a method of adapting the Linotype casting machine to the composition of music for printing typographically. The matrices have component parts of notes on them, and when the lines of metal are cast and brought together the complete notes and staves are formed. The method is said to be applicable to indenting stereo " flongs " and to producing movable type.

W. H. and C. H. Bolton, in a patent (No. 7430 of 1898), describe something like a rubber type outfit, with a self-inking stave ruler, set of punches, and an inking pad.

The rubber stamp idea repeatedly crops up in musical patents. F. M. Green, as early as 1872 (No. 3814), patents the idea of using rubber stamps with an inking pad and ruled paper, completing the characters with a pen, and adding characters rarely used.

Several inventors have endeavoured to simplify the printing by changing the system of the notation. J. F. Pitman, for instance, has a patent (No. 270 of 1857) in which he proposes to represent the notes by attaching letters to the stems instead of the usual heads. The letters are those representing the notes A, B, C, D, E, F, G. To distinguish the natural notes, he makes the lettered notes upright, whilst those for the sharps and flats are inclined to right and left respectively.

J. Lang, in his patent (No. 132 of 1868), has a similar object in view, but he retains the note heads, putting the initials of the name of the note in the Tonic Sol-fa system on the heads. On the black notes the letters are white and on the white notes they are black.

G. E. Morgan, in Patent No. 2345 of 1870, patents substantially the same idea, only the initials are those of the old notation.

H. Wagner, in Patent No. 10391 of 1892, proposes a new style of music notation which would make the engraving of music plates or the setting-up of music type delightfully simple if it were adopted. His idea is to dispense with stems and hooks, using only the heads. The white notes then represent the white keys of the pianoforte and the black notes the black keys. By sloping the notes in different directions, sharps, flats, and naturals are represented. Bar lines are used at equally spaced intervals, and the relative position of the notes illustrate the duration of the sounds. Rests are always marked by the same sign, and their duration is determined in the same way as

230

the notes. In printing music under this system, the inventor says the types or matrices have their breadth or their length exactly proportional to the duration assigned to the sounds or to the rests indicated by the signs they carry.

Another class of patents is that in which the inventors have sought to make the lines of the stave represent more clearly the position of the notes. For instance, the black lines are made to represent the black keys of the pianoforte, and the white spaces the white keys. An extra wide space between two staves represents the middle note C of the piano.

D. H. Shuttleworth-Brown (No. 18426, 1901) proposes to print the notes representing the black keys on the lines of the stave, and those representing the white keys in the spaces between.

The inventor, T. B. Harpur (No. 774 of 1864), proposes to print the various parts in different colours to facilitate reading. The different notes, tones, semi-tones, and other musical characters may also (he says) be printed in different colours.

E. Ball, in his Patents Nos. 12305 of 1890, 7620 of 1891, and 21599 of 1904, has a device in the form of a disc, through the centre of which is pushed a penholder, carrying a pen. Around the edge of the disc are the music characters in rubber type. Nothing is said about the staves, so we must assume they are already ruled on the paper. A small piece of sponge charged with ink is pressed against the disc, which is revolved until the character required is opposite the place where it has to be stamped on the paper ; then it is pressed down and revolved to another position. The impressions are evidently completed or touched up with the pen. A separate handle carries the signs for the G and F clefs.

G. Royle's invention (Patent No. 1167 of 1891) consists of a rectangular framework carrying two slides, one on guide rails. One slide carries a device for ruling the staves, and another has on it a number of push buttons, under which are the types for the various signs. The slide has a longitudinal and transverse motion, so that any sign can be brought to its correct position on the paper, which is held on the bed by means of a spring clip.

L. Durdilly (No. 5896 of 1892) patents a machine consisting of a table on which the paper is clamped, and is arranged to slide to and fro under a wheel which has type characters round its periphery. The wheel can be brought to the right position by means of a pedal, which also actuates the inking rollers. It is stated that the machine can also be used for preparing the plates employed in music printing.

L. C. and J. F. Badeau, in their patent (No. 22806 of 1905), claim for a typewriting machine for music, in which the type characters are carried by spring-controlled plungers, mounted in a disc which is rotated by depressing the keys, thus bringing the desired character into position for printing.

A prolific inventor of mechanical devices for printing music by a process of stamping is F. Dogilbert, of Brussels. His process was originated in Paris in 1905, and transplanted to Brussels in 1908. He has continuously perfected his method, and has demonstrated that it has qualities which assure its future. Thousands of plates have been made by this process, and in many cases the results have shown a greater perfection than hand engraving. Publishers in Brussels and Leipzig utilized the process considerably up to the day of declaration of the war.

M. Dogilbert has furnished the author with a description of his method, which we here summarize, and he has made the diagram of his machine printed herewith. Further details may be obtained from his English patents, Nos. 14337 of 1906 and 11811 of 1907. The method is termed electrogravure, and its initial principle is the creation of a record capable of being reproduced by photo-mechanical processes.

A coated white paper, ruled with squares in pale blue lines, is first employed to set out the arrangement of the music by apportioning the number of characters to the pages, and spacing out accordingly. The squares are proportioned to the size of type-body chosen, and facilitate equidistant spacing. The indications of the notes and signs are marked by conventional signs in blue pencil or ink and, being in blue, are not photographically reproduced. This preparatory work is analogous to that required as a preliminary to punching and engraving on pewter plates, but it has the following advantages—

(a) The work is drawn the right way round on the paper, whereas it would have to be reversed on a plate ; (b) it is on a white surface with blue ink or pencil, so that it can be readily seen ; (c) the square ruling with thickened lines to denote ten divisions permits of rapid laying-out, and avoids having to measure off the bar lines and other divisions with the compass.

The staves are printed successively, so that when the music presents any inequality of spacing due to the notes on ledger lines above or below the stave, this can be allowed for. The staves fall in register with the blue lines on the paper. The sheets thus prepared are put in the hands of copyists, who write the music of the manuscript on the staves by means of convenient signs, forming a sort of shorthand which is rapid and simple. They are guided in the spacing out by the indications marked on the manuscript by the chief engraver.

Finally, the sheets so prepared are given to the operator in charge of the stamping machine, which is provided with a punch representing the key, and this key is printed in the space where the operator finds it indicated on the " copy." The same routine is applied to all the signs often repeated—crotchets, quavers, minims, rests, etc., each falling in its proper place.

In order to avoid excessive complications due to the multiplicity of signs, only the frequently-recurring ones are stamped by the machine. The others are either drawn in or inserted by means of small labels pasted on to the sheet. The bars are put in by means of the ruling pen, and some of the signs are completed in the same way. Errors are corrected with a scraper, or with a brush applying a touch of blue colour over the required part.

The text and words are set up and printed typographically on bands of paper, and pasted in proper position under the staves. The operator, usually a girl, acquires great skill by constant practice, and can turn out quite a number of sheets per day.

It is only necessary to hand these sheets over to the photo-lithographer, who makes a wet collodion negative the desired size, and makes a blue print from it. This is sent to the publisher or author as a proof, so that any corrections or alterations can be indicated on it. If these corrections are extensive, they are best made on the original " copy " by pasting over certain portions and making a fresh negative ; or, if small, the corrections can be made on the zinc plate on to which the negative is printed. The pages are imposed four or more on a plate, as in ordinary printing ; and then the edition is run off on the lithographic machine.

Designs, title-pages, autographs, and pages of existing music can be imposed with the new " copy."

The arrangement of the punching machine will readily be understood from the accompanying diagram. (Fig. 103.) The operator holds the sheet of paper in position by both hands, and guides it in the free space between the punch and the table. At rest, the punch is kept up by the recoil spring, and the rollers are ready for inking when the magnetic core is drawn down towards the base by the closing of the electric circuit, which is accomplished by the pedal. This contact is only established for a moment, precisely when the sheet of paper is duly placed under the punch. This position is easily attained, because the paper is constantly attracted towards the table by means of a perforated ring surrounding the impression

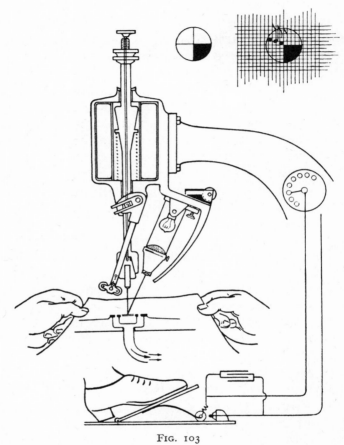

F𝗂ɢ. 103

DOGILBERT'S MUSIC STAMPING MACHINE

pad, and this suction has the effect of limiting the movement, imposing a sort of elastic drag. This also avoids doubling of the impression. The exact registering of the punch on the required square is obtained by means of an image of a cross-ruled screen projected on to the required spot by means of the electric lamp. This image can be easily seen even in a fully-lighted workroom.

The inking consists of a train of two rollers, which take ink from the cylinder and distribute it by their passage over the curved table towards the punch.

The machine for printing the staves presents the same mechanical characteristics, and is only a lateral amplification of the punching machine, without, however, the electrical mechanism, which would not be any advantage, owing to the few motions it has to accomplish. The index is a metallic guide instead of the optical screen image. The mandrel is provided with a long composing-stick in which the five-line rule pieces are inserted.

The inventor says he has made on an average 25 square metres (about 269 sq. ft.) of work per day by means of these machines.

A battery of these machines is being used regularly by a music printing firm in Brussels.

Another direction in which inventors have exercised great ingenuity is in the designing of type-writers for transcribing MS. music. The patent of H. & M. Wiedmer (No. 1620 of 1906) describes a pedal-operated platen shift for obtaining the stave position, the paper being carried on rollers above, and these rollers have horizontal and vertical movements. The machine has something like the ordinary typewriter keyboard, operating typebars. The same inventors have another patent (No. 27679 of 1906) for improvements on the above machine. The paper in this case moves over a flat impression surface. There is a carriage and shifting mechanism for obtaining the position of the notes.

G. M. N. Lafarie has a patent (No. 343 of 1908) for a typewriter with means for shifting the paper carriage to enable the characters to be written at the proper places on the staff. Each type bar carries two characters, either of which is brought into position by shifting the pivot of the typebar. Fourteen pianoforte keys are used to raise and lower the paper carriage within the limits of two octaves. In another patent by the same inventor (No. 3379 of 1908) for improvements on this machine, it is stated that four of the type keys are used to print ledger lines.

Some time before the late war, the Blick Typewriter Co. introduced a typewriting machine for music, and we give an illustration of it (Fig. 104), from which it will be seen that it has a very practical appearance. The company are not now selling this machine. A result we have seen of the work of the machine, executed on lithographic transfer paper, shows quite a good style of work, closely approaching the appearance of engraved music.

Another music typewriter which is on the market at the present time is based on the patents of the Rev. J. Walton, and is manufactured by The Music Typewriter Co., of Hatton Wall, London, E.C. The

FIG. 104
THE BLICK MUSIC TYPEWRITER

illustration (Fig. 105) shows the construction of the machine very clearly. It rules the staves; prints dense black notes, spaces, binds, headings, wording, etc., exactly like ordinary printed music. The operator can see the character and the line on which it is being printed before depressing the printing lever. The

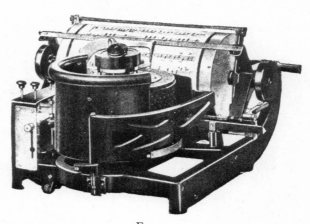

FIG. 105

THE WALTON MUSIC TYPEWRITER

machine is fitted with a transposing key, by which it automatically transposes as the operator copies, no expert knowledge being required. It is also claimed that the machine will print band and orchestral parts line for line at a similar speed to an ordinary typewriter. The type characters are attached to a revolving drum. By means of a simple appliance fixed to the type drum, the next stave required may be ruled in one operation and in any position as the carriage is returned to the starting point. The machine can be used for making lithographic transfers, or for making " copy " for the photo-engraver, or for preparing wax paper stencils for duplicating.

Several inventors have endeavoured to apply electrotyping and stereotyping methods to the production of music plates. E. J. N. Javin (No. 725, 1857) describes a process in which the characters are engraved on a sheet of tin on which guttapercha is poured or pressed to form a mould. Copper is deposited on this and, when a sufficiently thick shell has been obtained, it is backed up as usual with soft metal and mounted as a block. Another way is to take a stereotype direct from the metal sheet, or a plaster cast may be taken and the stereo or electro obtained from that.

J. D. Schneiter (No. 845, 1862) proposes that the characters should be produced in relief by means of transfer or other suitable ink on thin sheets of metal or other substance, etched and gummed over in the manner usual in lithographic printing. The characters thus formed may be separated and made to adhere to a lithographic stone or sheet of metal, so as to form a surface from which impressions may be at once obtained, or a transfer may be made on a litho stone or sheet of metal. By pressing, casting, electrotyping, or other means, a mould may be obtained, either from the plate with which the letters or other characters were imprinted on thin metal leaf, or from the movable leaf-metal type. It is claimed that the use of these thin metal sheets obviates the necessity of keeping in stock a large number of litho stones.

W. H. Lennox, J. W. & W. J. Pearman (No. 3840, 1868) describe the production of stereotyped plates for printing music either from stamped or embossed impressions on metal plates or from reversed engraved plates. In the first case, the lines of the staff are engraved at a proper distance apart on a plate of soft metal or alloy. The plate is then stamped with dies of the various designs necessary to produce on the plate the notes or symbols of music printing with the bars, etc., all reading the right way. A stereo, preferably of ebonite, is made from the stamped plate, and this prints the music the right way for reading. Or a plaster cast may be taken and the background cleared away until the representation of the plate is exposed to a raised surface reading the wrong way. A second casting surface produces sunken surfaces reading the right way, and from this a stereo may be obtained.

D. Colville (No. 2688 of 1869) proposes the production of a matrix which may be used for electro-typing or stereotyping by indenting or impressing suitable punches into the surface of a mould plate which is covered with wax or other plastic material. To obtain the impressions, he uses a sort of stamping press, and the moulding plate is adjusted for each note by means of a lever. The stave is ruled by a roller formed of five discs suitably spaced. The mould is kept heated.

P. M. Shanks (No. 1517, 1874) is the inventor of a method of hollowing out the matrix in a plaster composition by means of a rotating drill or cutter. This is on the same principle as the routing machine used by all photo-engravers at the present day. The matrix composition is made of china clay or similar substance mixed with starch or gum moulded into a block and dried. A block of plaster of Paris may be heated to about 180° F. and, when dry, immersed in an alcoholic solution of shellac. When saturated, the block is dried. Other resinous gums and solvents are mixed with it if desired, or paraffin wax may be used. Wood blocks or cylinders may be engraved by the same machine. The cutter is connected to the tracing point of a pantograph, so that a corresponding form may be employed as a guide, or the design may be engraved or sunk in gelatine. From the plaster matrix an electrotype or stereotype may be made.

C. Lourdel (No. 1445, 1874) stamps the notes on a sheet of metal, takes a proof and transfers to wood, which is engraved, and an electro taken from it. The separate notes are cut from the cast, and mounted by soldering or other process upon the extremities of shanks, preferably of zinc. In another process, wire is drawn through dies to give it the required section, and is cut into lengths of about ⅜ in., which are mounted on shanks. A third process proposed by this inventor is to cast types with the shank and character in one piece of metal, preferably zinc. A further process is to cast a piece of metal and strike the note on the extremity of it by means of a suitable die in a fly press. The notes are printed singly and by hand in a frame on to a sheet of paper. The bevelled edge of a sliding board serves as a guide. Words are printed on the same sheet or on bands of paper attached. Proofs are made in transfer ink on a sheet of zinc. Types for words or frequent signs are mounted in a handle.

Some inventors seem to have seen an opening for processes which can be used for printing music at home, when a limited number of copies are required. D. Gestetner in No. 7536 (1885) proposes to produce stencils for the stave lines by means of discs, with roughened or toothed peripheries mounted on a forked frame, with an axle to enable them to revolve. The notes are presumably to be written in with a stylus in the well-known manner adopted in the Cyclostyle and similar processes, the stencil then being inked and printed from.

E. Cremers (No. 10671, 1904) has a similar object in view. He proposes to use the stencil sheet for the Mimeograph, Cyclostyle, Neostyle, etc., in combination with a plate of celluloid having perforations corresponding to the musical symbols. A stylus is to be used through the perforations. This inventor also describes a device for ruling the staves.

R. E. Lee (No. 898, 1857) devises a portable press for printing from type, stone, copper, or steel, and a type case. These are constructed so that they can be carried, together with the requisite printing materials, in an ordinary workbox or dressing-case. The press comprises a bed and cylinder, which is reciprocated over the bed by means of nuts and worms actuated by bevel gear and a handle. The cylinder may be replaced by a little scraper.

G. Becker and D. Monnier (No. 10558, 1886) describe an instrument in the form of a beam calliper.

One needle point is set on the sheet to be copied, the second needle point being applied to the sheet to be printed. Beside this second needle point is a holder for type characters, which may be changed, or a wheel with characters on it may be employed. It is inked and pressed down.

M. A. Wier (No. 7527, 1886) has a frame on rollers, which runs over the music to be copied. A type wheel runs over the blank stave lines, and is turned to present the type required. Then it is depressed on to the paper. The frame which runs over the music to be copied is connected by tubes to a similar frame, which runs over the ruled paper above. Actuating mechanism runs through the tubes, so that when a key is depressed on the " copy " it turns a rack and pinion, which rotates the type-wheel and forces it down on to the paper. The type may be carried in a long comb instead of on a cylinder.

245

CHAPTER XX

APPLICATION OF PHOTO-MECHANICAL PROCESSES
TO MUSIC PRINTING

ATTEMPTS have been made from time to time, down to quite recently, to apply photo-mechanical methods to the reproduction of music, and at the present time some music printing firms are actually using processes in which photography plays a part.

We have traced a number of patents having this object, and it will be interesting to summarize them.

M. Alissoff, in Patent No. 591 of 1877, proposed to print musical signs or letters, preferably three or four times the usual size, on sheets of transparent paper ; or to cut out the signs from black or coloured paper, and to paste them up on a suitable background. From the original thus prepared, a reduction is made by photography, and the negative is employed for any of the usual photo-mechanical processess.

H. Goodwin, in Patent No. 3243 of 1878, describes how he proposes to make a background made up of stretched wires to represent the staves, the background and alternate wires being painted white. The intervening wires being black, correspond to the black lines of the stave. Notes are cut out of metal or wood painted black, and provided with flanges for attaching them to wires. If required, the black

246

and white may be reversed, the background being black and the notes white, so as to produce a negative result. Instead of wires, strips of white material can be let into the background, and the notes or signs having a flange which slides into a groove. The forme so set up is photographed, the negative printed on to a sensitized metal plate, which is developed, inked, and etched. The plate is then used for printing or is electrotyped.

J. P. Liorel, in Patent No. 22112 of 1902, describes how he proposes to construct a large scale model, prepared by ruling black lines on a board to represent the staves. Upon these lines are placed models of the notes and other signs cut out of thin wood, or other material, these having projecting points which may be pressed into the soft wood of the backboard, or the latter may have grooves in it. The whole is then reproduced by photography. As an alternative, it is proposed to use a metal plate instead of a board, and to arrange electro-magnets behind it, so that if the notes are in sheet metal they will adhere where placed until they are photographed.

The most recent invention on these lines is that of Mr. A. E. Bawtree (Patent No. 923 of 1915). He has the notes drawn on a large scale, then photographed so as to get, by printing on photographic bromide paper, a sufficient number of duplicates of the notes and signs. These are cut up and placed in a tray with compartments in the same way as type in a case. A sheet of glass is prepared, also by photography, with the staves on it printed in blue lines (which do not photograph when the final copying is done), which serve as guide lines. The paper notes or letters are made to adhere to the glass plate when they are laid in their places on the stave, the surface of the plate being adhesive. On completion of the whole page of music on the glass plate, a sheet of transparent paper bearing the black stave lines is attached to the plate in register with the blue lines, and it is put up in front of the camera for photographing. By lighting the plate with artificial light equally from the back and the front, the edges of the cut pieces of paper on which the letters are printed do not show in the photograph, and a clean negative results.

It will be seen that this process has some points of resemblance to that of Dogilbert, already described.

Bawtree has subsequently patented another method which could be adopted for music printing, although he does not claim this. His idea is to have the letters around a circular glass plate on which the letters are positive, and mechanism is provided for rotating the plate so that one letter at a time is brought opposite to an illuminated opening, which is opposite to the lens of a photographic camera, in which is a mechanism for shifting the plate step by step, so that the required lettering is built up on the photographic negative.

To avoid having to build up an original on a large scale and make a photographic reduction, other inventors have endeavoured to make a transparent negative or positive by stamping the notes the size required. For instance, in Patent No. 3369 of 1870, J. L. Davies describes how stamps with opaque ink may be applied to transparent paper to form a positive which could be used for photographic printing. He, however, mentions several alternative methods which are interesting as foreshadowing later inventions. He says that by stamping on transfer paper, the sheet may be transferred direct to stone ; or a sheet of paper may be chemically prepared and the design produced on it by passing an electric current through the type or punch pressed on to the paper. This latter method was some years afterwards patented by Mr. Friese Greene and exploited as " Electric Inkless Printing." Another way was to stamp the notes with a greasy ink, darken the surrounding parts by applying a photographically opaque varnish to the paper, and then wipe away the greasy ink, so that the lines were left translucent or transparent. This method was also repatented in later years by Ozias Dodge, and introduced (though not for music) under the name of the " Norwich Film " process. This inventor (J. L. Davies) seems to have conceived many ways of carrying out his ideas for superseding the use of the expensive pewter plates. He suggests that blocks of white wood might be stamped and the depressions filled in with black composition, the surface being then planed off, and copied photographically. The process might be similarly carried out by stamping through carbon manifolding paper ; also by stamping in soft metal, guttapercha, paper pulp, plaster, and taking a cast from the mould.

A patent (No. 8755, 1912), describes the ruling of stave lines with ink on a transparent sheet having vertical and horizontal hatching lines in transparent ink. The notes are sketched in pencil and afterwards put in with opaque ink by means of hand stamps. The sheet is used as a negative.

R. Tissington (No. 8504, 1889) has a process relating to the printing of music by means of types of metal or other material. The letters are set up and pasted on a support of glass or white paper or cardboard. This may be printed from direct or by photography if the glass support is used, and photo-lithographic transfers produced. In printing music direct from the types, the latter may be mounted type-high on wooden strips and combined with ordinary types for printing words.

At the present day a considerable amount of cheap music is produced by photo-lithography or photo-zincography, and by the photo-zinco block process. These terms may not convey much to the layman, and we will, therefore, briefly explain them. In photo-lithography, a negative is made of the sheet of music to be copied, and a print is made from this negative on to a sheet of paper coated with gelatine, made sensitive to light by bichromate of potash. When this print is inked all over with a roller, it is immersed in water, and lightly wiped with a tuft of cotton; the exposed lines are found to have taken up ink, whilst the surplus is cleared away from the white ground. This sheet then forms a transfer, which is put down on a lithographic stone and printed from in the usual manner.

Photo-zincography was formerly done in the same way, only that a sheet of zinc was used instead of stone as the printing surface. Of late, however, processes have been employed by which the image is printed direct from the negative on to the zinc plate, this being made sensitive to light in a similar manner to the transfer paper.

Another method of photo-zincography is the Vandyke process ; in this case, a printed sheet of music is used in place of the negative. The light acts through the paper on to the sensitized zinc plate, the black ink on the notes and lines stopping the light. The result is negative (i.e. white lines on a dark ground on the zinc), but by a simple process this is converted into a positive, and printing is then done in the usual lithographic manner.

During and since the late war, this process has been found very useful for reprinting music previously printed in Germany. The difficulty caused by the printing being on both sides of the sheet was ingeniously got over by splitting the paper, which is not such a difficult operation as it seems. One way is to paste a sheet of linen on each side of the music sheet ; when the paste is dry, a little knack acquired by practice enables the sheet to be split by drawing the pieces of linen away from each other. The paper is then soaked off and dried.

Where it is not possible to destroy the original music in this way, an ordinary photographic negative on glass may be made for printing down on to zinc. One London firm is making paper negatives by photographing the music in the camera on to a specially thin bromide paper, which is made translucent by treatment with paraffin wax.

251

Before the war, a German inventor was endeavouring to vend in England, for a very large sum of money, a process for copying old music even when it was bound in volumes, without taking the pages apart. He prepared a glass plate with a special sensitive emulsion, the secret of which was not divulged. When dry, this glass plate was laid, coated side down, on the page of music, and light was allowed to act on the plate. The theory of the process was that the white paper reflected light back through the plate and acted on the emulsion ; whilst the black lines of the music staves and notes reflected no light, and, therefore, had no effect. The result, by further treatment, was a negative which could be printed from on to a zinc plate. The method was not entirely original. It was a cleverly worked out application of a much earlier English invention by J. H. Player, who introduced it under the name of Playertype. Those who wish to know more about it may find particulars in the Patent Office, in back numbers of photographic journals, and in the author's book on *Line Engraving*.

The German process has since the war been acquired by a Swiss firm, who are running it successfully under the name of the " Manul " process, this title being a transposal of some of the letters of the name of the inventor, Ullman. The process has been introduced into England by Mr. J. J. Holme, of the Muston Co., London, and is being practically employed in music and text printing.

The photo-zinco block process consists of printing on the sensitized zinc plate direct from a negative, and when the print has been inked and developed, the lines are strengthened with acid-resisting material, such as by dusting with powdered resin or asphaltum ; then the plate is etched until the lines stand up in sufficient relief to be printed in the typographic presses. The firm of E. Marks & Son, Hackney, do a good deal of music printing in this way. They print four pages at once, mounting the plates on an iron bed, so as to get a good solid impression and for ease of replacing them on the machine.

The Collotype process has been used for reprinting very old music such as is found in museums and libraries. The value of this process lies in the facility with which it will reproduce with facsimile effect old, faded, and discoloured pages, or where there is coloured ornamentation. Collotype printing is done direct from thick glass plates having a gelatine coating, which is made sensitive to light. The effect of the exposure under a negative is that the printed lines take up ink, which can be renewed after each impression.

The " Anastatic " Process was formerly much used for reproducing music, and was worked with especial success in Germany. A sheet of printed music was moistened on the back by sponging with dilute acid, which had some effect of freshening the old ink, so that it could be transferred to stone, the printing being then done in the usual lithographic manner. If the paper was printed on both sides, it did not matter, as means were adopted to transfer first one side and then the other. As a rule, the original music was not damaged by the process.

CHAPTER XXI

SUMMARY OF THE PROCESSES USED IN
MUSIC ENGRAVING AND PRINTING

IT will be seen from the preceding chapters that almost every possible method of printing and of the kindred arts has been pressed into the service of the music printer.

The successive stages in the history of music printing may be summarized as follows—

1. Blank spaces left in the text for the music (both lines and notes) to be filled in by hand.

2. The lines printed with the text, but the notes left to be written in by hand.

3. Lines printed with the text, and the notes stamped in separately by hand.

4. Notes printed with the text, but the lines ruled by hand.

5. Notes and lines cut on a block and printed in the text as an illustration.

6. Notes and lines impressed by separate printings either from blocks or from type.

7. Notes and lines set up together in type and printed with or without text.

8. Notes, lines, and lettering engraved on copper and printed direct from the plate.

9. Notes, lines, and lettering punched on zinc, copper, or pewter plates, and printed direct from the plate.

10. Notes, lines, and lettering drawn on stone and printed lithographically.

11. Notes, lines, and lettering drawn on transfer paper and transferred to stone or zinc (latterly, also on aluminium), and printed lithographically.

12. Transfers pulled from the punched pewter plates, transferred to stone, or zinc, or aluminium, and printed lithographically.

13. Reproductions of existing music by photomechanical processes printed lithographically, or by collotype, or from photo-zinco blocks.

14. Utilization of stereotyping and electrotyping processes.

15. Printing of music by means of special typewriters.

CHAPTER XXII

THE POSITION OF BRITISH MUSIC ENGRAVING

WE may fittingly close our book with a few notes, which could not very well be included in the preceding chapters, on the present position of British music engraving.

Before the war, British music engraving and printing had sunk to a very low position. The English publishers, with a very few exceptions, preferred to send their work to Germany, primarily, no doubt, on the score of cheapness, though it was also claimed that the German engraved music was more elegant in appearance. This may have been so in the early days of the art, but skilful British engravers have succeeded in producing work which was indistinguishable for elegance and clearness from the foreign product.

It was also urged that, owing to the limited number of British engravers, it was not possible for them to produce the quantity of work required. That, however, is a statement which the British engravers deny, and they point to the fact that during the war they were able to produce all the plates required, in spite of depleted staffs owing to many of the younger engravers joining the Army. Of course, publishers curtailed considerably their publications, but this probably only reduced the engravers' work proportionately to the diminution in the number of engravers.

After the war, when commercial relations had again been opened up with Germany, a few publishers recommended sending work to Germany in order to get the advantage of cheapness through the low rate of exchange, but the imposition of the Reparations Duty checked this somewhat. Work is still going to Germany, but the Customs officials see that the words " Printed in Germany " appears on each piece. This, no doubt, acts as a deterrent.

It is conceded that the music engraving trade is now in a much better condition than before the war, and the workmen are better paid. In 1914, the trade union for all official purposes gave the average wage of music engravers as £2 10s. per week of fifty hours, but a quick and experienced workman could command £3 per week. The earnings differed considerably : where one man would earn 1s. 3d. per hour, another would only earn 10d. To-day, of course, the wages are higher in common with those in most other trades.

The British engravers have not now the competition of the German workmen who came over here before the war. It is admitted they were good workmen, as they should be, from the excellent training they were able to get in the large music printing houses in Germany.

Though at one time the German workmen excelled the British engravers, yet at the time of the outbreak of war there was not much to choose between a good British engraver and a German one. This may have resulted from the fact that the German and British engravers often worked side by side, and were on good terms with each other, so that it was possible to compare methods of working. If anything, the Britisher was in many cases preferred by the German firms who started music engraving and printing over here, the British engravers being entrusted with the best work.

In one respect, the German workmen had the advantage at first in that they had the best tools. There were then no British makers of music engraving tools, but the German workmen helped their British fellow-workers to get the proper tools, and thus the superiority of the German engraver's work became less evident, until there was no essential difference.

On the outbreak of war, there was an exodus of the German engravers back to their own country, and the few who preferred to remain were soon interned, so that the British engravers have been left in possession of the field.

As there are probably not more than 100 music engravers in the whole kingdom, and there is now much more work to be done at home, there should not be any unemployment in this industry. In fact, there was a demand for good engravers that could not be supplied for some time after the war ended, but the general trade depression has considerably altered conditions at the time of writing.

It is certain that if this country is to take a foremost place in music engraving, many more apprentices will have to be trained than hitherto. In the past, the rules of the trade union have restricted the number of apprentices, but during the war these rules were relaxed, and the situation has improved, over fifty apprentices have been taken into the trade during the last six years.

The rule formerly was one apprentice to five men, now one to three or four men are allowed, according to the size of the shop. Some of the shops have employed so few men, either through depletion due to the war or through inability to get any more, that such a relaxation of the rule was necessary to enable an extra apprentice to be employed.

We are informed that it usually takes at least two years before an apprentice can do even moderately good work, and not till he has been practising for about four years does he begin to show any real signs of proficiency. Only lads of a very special temperament are suited for the work at all ; many have not the patience to go through the drudgery of the initial training. The work is not hard, but it is tedious, and the slowness with which skill is acquired is at first discouraging.

One employer informed us that the physical and mental strain on a lad who takes the business seriously is such that it is often found best to let him take a rest or have some recreation for a time to get into a fit state for doing the work. Some engravers who have not felt any such strain in the days of their apprenticeship may think this is an exaggerated case, but it may be that some do not feel the effects so much as others. Good eyesight is one of the essentials of fitness for the work, as the engravers do not use the eyeglass or hand magnifier as in other kinds of engraving. The work being comparatively bold, it is not considered that any such aid is necessary. After a time, as the work becomes more natural, it is done without any great effort, and to an experienced engraver becomes almost perfunctory.

Before the war, the master engravers thought that the trade union did not encourage the training of apprentices ; and when it was first proposed to start a class for music engraving at one of the technical institutes, so many objections were raised, that the London County Council, which was ready to start a class, had to abandon the idea for a time, feeling that they could not proceed without the full support of the trade. Matters have improved since the war, and a class for music engraving has been running since 1920 at the Central School of Arts and Crafts.

Another way in which the shortage of engravers has been met is by the large music printing firms appointing one of their engravers to act as special instructor to the apprentices they employ.

A large firm of music printers, whose opinion was invited on this subject, said—

We have a difficulty in getting engravers, and herein lies the trouble for the British employers. If the training of British lads to engrave music plates was taken up seriously and a number of pupils were steadily turned into the trade, the other parts of the work are quite within our grasp. Get a market for engravers and there will be plenty of work for them. We could undertake more work, but we must first get the engravers ; then we can get more litho machines, and there is nothing to hinder British firms from holding British work. We are impressed by our weakness on the engraving side of the business.

In France and Belgium, women are engaged in the

work of punching, and the more difficult part of engraving is left to the men ; but it is said that women are not successful in producing the best work. If an attempt were made to introduce women into the work in this country, it is most probable that the men would resist the innovation, so that there is not much hope of solving the labour difficulty by that means.

One circumstance that has stood in the way of improvement in the music engraving trade is that the prices for the work are very low. The trade price—that is to say, the price charged by the master engraver to the publisher—for engraving a page of pianoforte music before the war was 4s. or 5s., exclusive of the cost of the plate, which might be from 1s. 3d. upwards, according to the quality of the metal. The working engraver would receive from 2s. 9d. to 3s. 6d. for his part of the work. It is obvious that high wages could not be earned at such prices, and, indeed, it was only by skilful handling that the work could be done at such a low cost. The prospect for youths entering the business was not, therefore, encouraging.

Considering the evidently tedious and intricate nature of the work, it is certainly done with surprising speed by skilful engravers. There cannot, of course, be any standard as to the time taken to engrave a plate, as so much depends on the character of the music and the skill of the workman. Naturally, the plates for such a work as Beethoven's " Sonatas " would take a much longer time to engrave than those for a simple ballad.

Engravers specialize on different classes of engraving.

Only the very best engravers can do a full score plate or the back page of a piece of music. This latter is the advertisement of the publisher, and usually has on it a number of small specimens of music showing the " theme."

The engraving of title-pages is a business in itself, and is done by a different class of men to the regular music engraver. It is a work requiring considerable taste and skill.

The introduction of mechanical methods of engraving is not looked upon by the trade as likely to greatly increase the output or to cheapen production. It is pointed out that music engraving is fundamental and not susceptible of being replaced by mechanical means. Even Tessaro's method, described elsewhere, which one of the leading engravers admitted worked well, was not so economical as hand work, even when girls were put on the machine.

As regards the printing of music, there can be no question that there are ample facilities in this country for producing all the music needed and of a quality quite equal to the foreign product.

If only British professors and teachers will drop their absurd preference for German-printed music, there is no reason why any more of the latter should come into this country. If German publishers want English editions, they should be compelled to have them printed here, so that British capital and labour may be usefully employed.

INDEX

INDEX

INDEX